CRASH

CRASH

How I Became a Reluctant Caregiver

RACHEL MICHELBERG

SHE WRITES PRESS

Published 2021
Printed in the United States of America
Print ISBN: 978-1-64742-032-1
E-ISBN: 978-1-64742-033-8
Library of Congress Control Number: 2020914018

For information, address:
She Writes Press
1569 Solano Ave #546
Berkeley, CA 94707

Interior design by Tabitha Lahr

She Writes Press is a division of SparkPoint Studio, LLC.

There are as many versions of every family's history as there are family members. This is mine. Some names of people and places have been changed.

For the caregivers.

"Life's challenges are not supposed to paralyze you;
they're supposed to help you discover who you are."
—BERNICE JOHNSON REAGON

"You don't have to choose how you're going to die or when.
You can only decide how you're going to live."
—JOAN BAEZ

"God gave burdens; he also gave shoulders."
—YIDDISH PROVERB

Prologue

SEPTEMBER, 2013

I throw the diamond in the trash.

Not on purpose. For X-rays before abdominal surgery, I'm instructed to remove my clothes and all jewelry. Last, I unclasp the necklace made with the diamond from my engagement ring. *I should put this in my purse.* But I'm agitated about going under the scalpel and it goes in the plastic bag with white handles, along with shoes, blouse, bra, and purse.

Kaiser is terrible at recycling, I'm thinking as I throw the bag away after the procedure. *So wasteful. I ought to write a letter.*

Stepping out of the shower the next morning I catch the reflection of my bare neck through the foggy mirror. I see my diamond in the plastic bag with the white handles, the bag in the trash can. I see an orderly emptying the can into one of several dumpsters behind the hospital.

I have thrown David away. Again.

Chapter 1

I was engaged three times before I finally married David, number four.

Number one was my college sweetheart. Number two was a jazz pianist, an academic.

Number three was Kenny the Surgeon. I was madly in love. He was smart, funny, not very tall but attractive in a Jewish doctor kind of way. At best the relationship was rocky. Kenny wouldn't make the commitment. I'd fume and leave; he'd beg to have me back, withdraw again; I'd get pissed and break up. We were in breakup mode when a friend called. Was I interested in meeting her coworker?

"He's tall and cute, with blue eyes. He's Jewish. Grew up in Germany. Didn't you spend some time there?"

"Good timing. Give him my number."

David and I had a nice chat a few days later. He was delighted that I knew German and invited me to practice. I'd become rusty and was embarrassed.

He picked me up for a dinner date a few days later. Over carpaccio and veal marsala at a sweet little Italian bistro in Palo

Alto, he told me what it had been like growing up in Munich in the '60s as a Jew—how he'd learned to be suspicious of gentiles, the *goyim*. About his father Samuel, who had lost his whole family in the Holocaust but survived Auschwitz and the Death March. Samuel met Maria, a Bavarian Catholic farm girl, in a displaced persons camp on the outskirts of Munich. She was working with the orphans. They'd divorced after years of Maria raising their three children almost single-handedly while supporting the whole family.

"Our mother wasn't Jewish and we were never really accepted by the Jewish community, so Sigi and Dora—my brother and sister—and I converted back, to preserve the identity the world had pinned on us," he explained. "We were learning to survive our own alien world."

My turn: I was a little embarrassed by my comfy suburban childhood in nearby Sunnyvale. But I was enthusiastic about my role in *Norma*, the opera I was rehearsing. "I also have two day jobs. I do administrative work for a Jewish charity, and I'm a synagogue cantor. That's more of a nights and weekends thing though."

"Wait, did you sing at the Holocaust Memorial service last year?"

"The one in Saratoga? Yes, I was the one who sang in Hungarian." I grimaced. "Definitely not in my cadre of comfortable languages."

"I was there! I thought you were so hot —but I didn't think it would be appropriate to hit on the cantor."

We laughed. This would be a story retold with delight.

As first dates go, it was good. He was smart, attractive, attentive. He drove an older chocolate-brown Mercedes convertible. His lilting, soft Bavarian accent was seductive, and his exotic European stories promised me access to the world beyond

Silicon Valley. Most important, he wanted to see me again. This could be alright.

Later that week Kenny showed up with a ring. I left David a voicemail, thanking him again for the dinner, but I was terribly sorry it wasn't going to work out. I don't remember mentioning that I'd become engaged.

David didn't let me forget that I'd broken up with him once via voicemail. In fact, he brought it up whenever people asked how we met. I always tried to add context ("Well, we'd only had one date"). "I'm just teasing," he'd say. I wasn't amused.

Six months later my relationship with Kenny was capsizing when I ran into David in the parking lot of a gourmet grocery store in Woodside. And I looked it—makeup-less, puffy-eyed, baggy sweats, unwashed ponytail. By the time I saw him it was too late—he'd seen me. I wanted to crawl under a BMW and hide.

"Oh hi!" I chirped, despite my despondent mood. My actress persona was professionally trained.

David's grey-blue eyes were wide and welcoming. If he noticed how disheveled I looked, he didn't let on. Pressed jeans, classy shoes, button-down shirt and blazer: *he* showed well.

"Rachel! How are you? What are you doing here?"

How much did I want him to know? "I live here now." I'd moved in with Kenny, though later that day I would move out.

David cocked his head and gazed at me. "You OK?"

I felt my mouth tightening against tears. I wanted to blurt out the operatic drama of my pathetic love life. I wanted to throw myself in his arms. I wanted him to adore me as willingly as Kenny was surgically unwilling.

Legs like jelly, I leaned against the BMW for support. "A little stressed right now." I forced a smile. "I'm OK." *Am I a performer or a good liar?* "It's good to see you." *I have to get out of here.* "Well, it was nice running into you. *Tschuss!*" I chirped, calling up the casual German word for goodbye. I felt David's eyes on me as I zig-zagged through the lot to my little blue Honda Civic.

Tears erupted in huge, choking sobs as I wound the hilly road back to Kenny's place to finish packing. I'd never felt so alone. All of my failures had collected into a giant, asphyxiating ball pressing on my chest. My fantasy life as a surgeon's wife— and probably anyone's wife—was over. I wailed and gasped for breath, driving the windy road by rote.

I mourned Kenny for several months. And then I called David.

·—·—·—·—·

David wants to take me flying—it's his passion. He's been taking lessons and recently earned his private pilot's license, allowing him to fly with passengers when the visibility is good. Flying off to lunch in Santa Rosa is intriguing. But I'm reluctant—not afraid exactly, but I detest that clutching in my stomach when there's a big drop. I haven't been on a roller coaster since my brother and sister dragged me onto the Giant Dipper at the Santa Cruz Boardwalk when I was nine. But I want to show David I'm adventurous, open to new experiences.

David is careful in the preflight check. As I help him get the plane ready, I feel very daring breaking out of my comfort zone. He's rented a low-wing airplane—the view isn't as good, but it will be more stable.

The weather is beautiful. Seeing so many familiar places from that perspective is breathtaking, despite the wings.

"There's Mount Diablo," he says. "And pretty soon you'll see the Benicia Bridge."

I feel very grown up—headset, jetting off to lunch, my tall blue-eyed European date.

A few weeks later David suggests a longer excursion: to Monterey. A bit pricey—in addition to the $300 plane rental, we'd need a car to get around to the tide pools at Point Lobos, dinner in Carmel.

I barely give Kenny a thought as David and I watch otters playing in the surf and stroll Ocean Avenue hand-in-hand. David encourages me to have a glass of wine with dinner but for him, he says, "No alcohol within eight hours of flying."

His adherence to the rules is comforting.

We arrive back to the Monterey airport late. It's already getting dark. Though David's license permits him to fly at night, I can see he's worried.

"Is something wrong?"

"Coastal fog coming in."

"Is that a problem?"

"Not sure yet."

It's now completely dark. Where there had been a few high clouds earlier, a thick, soupy fog billows past the few pole lights in the airport parking lot. Though it's a Sunday evening—normally a high-traffic time—the airport is completely deserted.

"It's a high-wing plane. You told me they weren't as stable. Should we drive home?" I don't really want to. Besides the expense of renting the car for another day, it will be a pain in the ass to retrieve the plane. And we both have to be at work early the next morning.

"No, we'll be OK." He doesn't look at me. I watch him perform the preflight check in complete silence—uncharacteristically. I'm shivering in the damp cold.

We board and put on our headsets. I can see nothing except blackness and thick white mist. Carl Sandburg's poem erupts in my mind:

The fog comes on little cat's feet.

It sits looking over harbor and city

on silent haunches
and then moves on.

May it move on.

Within a minute of taking off, the fog tightens around us like swaddling. It's anything but calming. The plane shakes violently, rattling and bucking like the Giant Dipper.

I'm going to die. We're going to crash, and we'll both die.

"Monterey Approach, this is Cessna four-two-niner-bravo, en route to San Jose. I am disoriented. Please advise. I am disoriented."

Possibly the worst thing I've ever heard.

Please. Please don't let us die. Please. I want to see my mother. I want to sing Carmen again. I want to have children.

The rattling and shaking intensifies. It is complete whiteout. I'm trapped in a cage that's being throttled by a pair of giant evil hands.

Not exactly cat's feet.

"Cessna four-two-niner-bravo, maintain visual flight rules. You are not cleared for flight in instrument conditions," I hear the voice crackle into my headset. *Jesus. We're about to die a fiery death, and David is being scolded.* "Turn left heading 080, direct Salinas, climb and maintain 3000 feet."

David clutches the yoke. As suddenly as we entered the fog bank, we're gliding through a black starless night. The fog below us is like a white shroud. Except for the whirr of the Cessna engine, all is quiet.

We fly in silence for the remaining thirty minutes. In silence we land and close down the plane. We drive back to David's apartment, where I've left my car.

I want to go home. I don't want to sleep with him—not even be in the same room. I'm not angry—I can see that David is punishing himself plenty. He's sick with embarrassment and guilt, barely looks at me. Still I want to get away. I have no idea what to say. For sure I can't comfort him.

But I stay that night in the awkward silence. I want to show that I'm compassionate, nurturing.

That I won't abandon him when things got rough.

A few weeks later David reluctantly shows me a letter from the FAA. His license is being temporarily suspended, pending further investigation.

"I'm sorry," I say.

But I'm not.

— ·—·—·— —·—·

David proposes on Valentine's Day, 1995. No surprise—we've been talking about getting married almost since the day we reconnected. He's thirty-five, I'm fast approaching that benchmark. We're both ready. Über-ready.

Red roses arrive at work with a note: "Can't wait until tonight. Happy Valentine's Day, I love you."

I'm excited but roll my eyes. I'm not very sentimental. I find the whole cultural mandate a bit trite, but the date means a lot to him so I play along.

He picks me up at my apartment, promptly drops down on one knee, and performs the routine. We have a reservation at the Flea Street Café, a trendy bistro in Menlo Park. It's loud, crowded, stifling. But that night to the besotted lovers, none of it matters.

The ring has a small, solitaire diamond. It's perfect. We'd researched diamonds together, learning about the 4 Cs: cut, color, clarity and carat. I opted for perfect clarity, but nothing showy. Class and taste. Simple but elegant.

As we settle into our tiny table, David is excited to share his epic travails of acquiring the ring. He'd purchased it through

Susanna—a childhood friend from Germany, who works for a diamond broker in Miami. She could get us a much better price than the local mall store—plus the quality assurance David wanted. His suspicious streak covered *goyim* working at Zale's in the mall.

Susanna sent the ring via UPS to David's high-tech office because he's worried that he won't be home to receive the package during the day. February 12th arrived, no package. The next day, still nothing. He's a nervous wreck. On the 14th, he practically camps out in the mailroom, but somehow misses the delivery. We have a great laugh over how he prowled the floors searching for the tiny package, always a step or two behind the mail cart. Pure slapstick.

When David finally retreats to his cubicle, desperately worried—not to mention his botched proposal plans—the miniscule $4,000 manila envelope is innocently sitting on his chair. The day is saved.

At the synagogue on Friday nights during the rabbi's sermon I extend my left hand, rotating it to catch the light, reveling in the sparkle. I love that ring. And I'm finally engaged. To a nice, smart, tall Jewish man with a good job. One who looks forward to children. Who adores me. I'm going to be alright.

We marry in August, 1995. The ring sparkles as we laugh through the early, loving years, the birth of our children, the surprise fifth anniversary trip to the Hotel Del Coronado in San Diego. Kid-free for a few days, we rent a red Mustang convertible and meander around La Jolla, I in my floppy hat and David with his arm flung across the back of my seat, relaxed and happy, telling stories about his year in San Diego on a Fulbright scholarship. We eat, make love, lie in the sun, shop for souvenirs for the kids.

My perfect simple diamond stays hidden at the bottom of my jewelry box during the awful years—the lawsuits, my hospitalizations, family feuds, stalking and vandalism, Mom's illness and death. From time to time I fish it out, remembering the proposal, the laughter, the promise of young love.

February 2005, two months before the crash.

Chapter 2

———————————————

April, 2005

On a warm spring evening, I am introducing the TV show *Little House on the Prairie* to seven-year-old Hannah.

Wise, fiddle-playing Pa, stern but fair. Loving, attentive Ma. Adversity: grasshoppers devouring crops, frigid Wisconsin winters, Mary going blind. Yet the Wilders are always a loving family, a functional family. Hardships only bring them closer together.

Every episode ends happily.

Pa is gently reprimanding Laura when the phone rings. I drag myself off of the sofa. I can hear Joshie in his room playing JumpStart Around the World. Six years old and always on the computer. Just like his dad.

"Mommy, hurry up," Hannah instructs as I head toward the kitchen. "You're going to miss it."

"I'll be right back, honey. It's probably Daddy calling to tell me they've landed and he's on his way home." Closing down the rented plane requires a long checklist of duties. He'll be an hour.

"Hello?"

"Rachel?" The guttural R identifies the caller as Israeli. "This is Dror Salee. I work with David."

"Oh, yes, hi, Dror." David had mentioned him several times. They got along well.

"There's been an accident."

I fall into a chair, pushing aside Joshie's unfinished milk to lean my elbows on the table. "Wait. What kind of accident?"

"The plane has gone down. In a vineyard. David's at a hospital in Paso Robles. So is Yaron. They're both in critical condition."

Is David paralyzed? Disfigured? At least he's not dead. But is he dying? How the hell does anyone even survive a plane crash?

I don't know what to ask. The room is spinning.

"Rachel? Are you still there?"

"Y-yes."

Dror speaks rapidly, as if he's afraid he might lose me altogether. "I guess they found my business card in David's wallet, that's why they called me first. Maybe you can ride down with Yaron's wife Miri. She's pregnant. Her friend is driving."

"Yes, I mean no, I mean that's probably a good idea." I stare at the cup of milk. "When is she leaving? I have to get someone to watch my kids. Oh my God. Oh. My. God."

"MOMMY!" Hannah is standing in the kitchen doorway, hands on princess pajama-clad hips. "Are you coming?"

She can't see this. I turn my back to her. "Just a second, Dror." I put my hand over the mouthpiece. "Go back in the living room, honey. I'll be right there."

She purses her lips and retreats. We both know I'll take longer than promised.

Dror will call back with details within the hour. I look around our cozy kitchen. The wall clock shows 8:20.

I dial my sister. She'll be over as soon as she can, will stay as long as necessary. I tell the kids to turn off the TV and computer,

override their protests for once. They wander into the bedroom
I share with David, ready for a bedtime story. I'm frantically
throwing random clothes into an overnight bag.

"Aunt Lisa is coming to read to you tonight. I have to go
away for a little while." I'm great behind a script or libretto, but
I've had no rehearsals for the lines I need. "A friend of mine is
sick." *Yes, that's good. Don't scare them with the truth, whatever
that may be.*

They snuggle into our bed looking at the books they've
brought. Dror calls—Miri and her friend will pick me up at about
9:15. Lisa looks grim when she arrives, asking for details I don't
have. She's left a meeting at the Unitarian church to be here.

"Please. Just distract the kids. They're settled in for a story."

Lisa's boys are a few years older than mine. She knows kids.
"Of course." She tries to smile, glances at the books scattered on
the bed. "C'mon guys, how about *Magic Tree House?*"

The doorbell chimes. I give the kids a quick hug. "Love you
both. See you soon." Lisa and I exchange glances.

After tense greetings, Miri and her friend continue in
hushed Hebrew for most of the three-hour ride. I leave several
messages at the clinic. I sit alone and panicky in the dark back
seat. A nurse finally calls back.

"Mrs. Mitch–el-berg?" she pronounces it wrong. They
usually do.

"It's Michael, like the man's name. Michelberg," I say,
annoyed, as if she should intuit the correct pronunciation.

"Your husband is very critical. There's severe damage to his
skull. Most likely internal organs as well. We're a small hospital.
We don't have a neurosurgery service, so we're transporting him
to San Luis Obispo."

Brain surgery?

"We're just trying to keep him alive."

Oh my God.

"Get here as soon as you can."

I tell Miri and her friend what I've learned. She's also been on the phone. Yaron is not as critical as David, but he has severe back injuries. He'll stay at the Paso Robles clinic. They understand that David's trauma is more critical, so they'll take me on to San Luis Obispo then return to Paso Robles to see Yaron.

I call my brother Paul. He insists on driving from Mill Valley, north of San Francisco—to meet me at the hospital. I call the rabbi who happens to be my boss at the synagogue where I'm the cantor: I won't be at work the next day. I ask him to pray for us, even though Jews don't usually do that. I stare out the car window into the blackness; there's no beauty of the spring-green hills to distract me.

At 1:30 a.m., we pull up to the ER at Sierra Vista Regional. I scramble out of the car after a quick thanks to Miri and her friend. I promise to keep in touch.

"You have my husband, David Michelberg?"

The ER receptionist directs me to the ICU. The tiny waiting room is empty. "Please ring the buzzer for service" reads a sign on the wall next to the door. The ICU door opens, and I rush inside.

A nurse stops me outside a curtained area and puts her hand on my shoulder. "Mrs. Michelberg, I need to warn you. You may not recognize him."

ICUs have a timeless quality, like casinos—hushed voices, constant motion, lots of noise. The whoosh of respirators. Rhythmic beeping of monitors, like a semi backing up. *Watch out, your life is moving in reverse.*

I know he'll be bandaged and swollen, connected to machines and IVs. *Gray's Anatomy* is my current can't-miss show. Before that *ER* and *St. Elsewhere*, so I'm somewhat of a trauma expert.

Beep, beep. I nod. "I understand."

When she pulls the curtain aside, it's clear I hadn't understood at all.

Someone gasps—me—my hand shooting to my mouth in revulsion. Nothing like *ER*. David's mottled face has blown up like a red beach ball. Tubes run everywhere—into his swollen mouth, both arms, and snake out of the top of his blood-soaked, bandaged head. Elephant Man with tubes. Tube Man.

Seriously, Rachel. Do something. Talk to him. Hold his hand. Tell him you're here. Can he hear anything?

I take a tentative step toward the bed, clearing my throat. Before I can speak one of the machines starts beeping a fast staccato. A small army rushes toward him. Someone yanks me back toward the waiting room. "He's coding. You need to wait outside."

"Coding?" *Shit. I know what that means.*

The door closes. The click is quiet but effective. I'm shut out. Blocked from the chaos. Banished into aloneness, isolation.

What am I supposed to do while my husband is dying? I don't know this role. Read a magazine? I sink into a chair. My head drops into my hands. With my pinkies I rub my forehead. In *Gray's Anatomy*, the wife always cries. But my eyes are dry. Because I'm uncaring? Because I don't love David enough?

Damn. I'm supposed to meet Mark for lunch. I need to tell him I can't make it. Tell him that David has been in a plane crash. Might already be dead. That I might be single. Available. Just like that.

The steel door opens. I jerk my head up. "David's been stabilized. Still in the induced coma. We're not sure when he'll be conscious, it could be a while."

Jesus Christ. How despicable to be thinking that I might now be free to be with Mark. Maybe there is a God—a vengeful God. A God making David pay for my adultery.

Punish me, God, not him. Please.

I picture his swollen face, the bloody bandages.

Mark is a musician in a local symphony. Not exactly the New York Philharmonic, but a respected second-tier orchestra. I had hired him to play the Kol Nidre—the prayer for annulling vows before God, at our synagogue's Yom Kippur service. The previous summer Mark had started dropping by the synagogue more often than necessary. We'd sit in my office and talk. I'd try not to let him see me glancing at his tanned, muscled forearms exposed by a button-down shirt rolled up to the elbows. Or his sensuous dark hair and mustache, his bottomless brown eyes. Then off-site coffees. Lunches, supposedly to discuss an upcoming concert of Handel's *Solomon*, or the chamber music piece based on *The Diary of Anne Frank* we were developing to perform in schools.

I've looked forward to seeing him. Flirting is fun. Risky, but surprisingly satisfying. Beyond the tedium of my everyday world. Acceptable as long as there's no touching. We only talk.

"Who's your absolute favorite composer?"

"Puccini," I admit, a little sheepishly. Puccini's considered a little cheesy by serious musicians, but oh so romantic—those soaring melodies, tragic love stories.

But Mark only smiles. "Mine is Brahms." Masculine, perfect musical structure, rich harmonies. So incredibly sexy that he loves Brahms.

We open up to each other. I tell him of my growing frustrations with David, who sleeps late, answers every question with a sarcastic comment, shirks housework. Gets lost in video games. Teases constantly despite my pleas to stop. Still smokes after years of proclaiming he's quit. He's a good dad, plays and bike rides with the kids, but I shoulder most of the parenting and housekeeping.

And I hear about Diane, older by eight years. A financial advisor who essentially supports them, since they can't live solely on a musician's income in Silicon Valley, well, not and drive a Lexus home to live in a country club. They sometimes still connect over late-night Scotch but he's not in love with her anymore.

Mark stops by to drop off some Handel scores for me to copy bowing marks into the string instrumental parts. David's working, the kids are at school. I'm making him a cup of tea in the kitchen. "Shouldn't we admit that something's going on here?" I blurt out.

He's startled, then takes me in his arms. "Yes, there's definitely something going on here."

We make our way to the sofa. As we kiss I'm more mortified about the smell of cat piss on the sofa than I am about making out with a man who's not my husband. *As long as you don't have sex, it's not really cheating, right?*

Denial is a handy state of being. You can do almost anything you want.

"This will end badly," Mark says, playing with my hair. "Diane can be very vindictive."

But Diane and David seem very far away at that moment. Still, we agree not to have contact for at least a month. "Cold turkey," I say. I'll work on my relationship, persuade David we need to see a counselor. My marriage is worth saving. He's a good guy, a loving father. We have two kids and a cat and a cute little house. I'm not going to wreck our lives with my silly infatuation.

Three weeks later we fall off the wagon. Still no sex, but our emails, phone calls, meetings became more frequent. I'm falling in love.

As I'm sliding down that slope, David falls out of the sky.

Chapter 3

I'M ALONE IN THE TINY WAITING room: me, outdated copies of *People* magazine, and the clock piercing every passing second into my awareness. The worn blue overnight bag is flaccid. Not even a decent book to drag me from this nightmare. As if I could concentrate.

I stare at the door into the ICU. Who knows what surprises lay behind it or what news will come through it? It's like *Let's Make a Deal,* that awful game show from the '70s that I had loved as a kid, home sick from school. If you choose the right door your future will be fabulous. A washing machine! A new car!

A dead husband.

But I have no choices, other than to wait. And wait. I'm stuck in an overheated cell with no company except the hum of the fluorescent lights.

When my brother Paul arrives I fall into his arms and he hugs me long and hard, all powerfully comforting 6'5" of him. He takes control like the TV and film producer he is. Peppers me with questions: What are the chances of David surviving? If he lives, will he be paralyzed? How did the crash happen—was it pilot error? He knows as little as I do. I tell him that Yaron had been piloting. David's license had lapsed.

For the next few hours there are no answers. I'm a wild creature, trapped, desperate for information that doesn't arrive. Paul and I hold hands, speculate. He drinks coffee from a thermos. The mixture of adrenaline, fear, and sleep deprivation fuels my pacing. I start a mental to-do list: cancel the Passover Seder we are hosting in two (or is it three?) days, arrange for someone to get Hannah to her piano lesson, let my former choir director know I wouldn't make the rehearsal that night for her anniversary concert.

At some point I look Paul straight in the eye. "I don't know if I should want him to live, or hope that he dies. What kind of life can he have with that kind of injury?"

What kind of life can I have?

Around five in the morning someone hands me release forms to sign for David's treatment: surgery within the next few hours, more to follow over the next few days. We're advised to get some rest.

Paul finds us a double room at a decent motel a mile or so away. The sun is hinting at rising as we check in. "My husband was in a plane crash. This is my brother," I explain to the lady at the registration desk. *Where is that coming from?* Perhaps I don't want her thinking there's something fishy going on. Why do I care if a stranger might judge me when my whole world is disintegrating? Is she sensing Mark's hold on my psyche?

The clerk tries to look sympathetic. "I'm sorry." She peers again at her computer screen. "How many nights will you be staying?"

I turn to Paul, he shrugs. "We don't know. Let's just start with tonight, well, this morning."

She hands us a key card. Paul picks up our bags. "Can we have a late checkout please?"

After a few hours of agitated sleep we drive back to the hospital. I gaze out the window at the seemingly normal mid-morning hum of the picturesque coastal town. Delivery trucks turning into driveways, a woman sipping a latte coming out of Starbucks, empty school buses returning from their morning rounds. Life goes on.

Does it?

At least we know David must be hanging on, since we'd been assured they'd call if there was a turn for the worse. Still, who knows what could be happening right now? Or in five minutes?

The hospital parking lot is much busier midmorning. We have trouble finding a parking spot. I want to scream at everyone that our needs are more important. My husband is much sicker. They should all clear out of the way.

David is coming out of surgery. The ICU nurse tells us that the surgeon will fill us in on the details. In a hallway lined with gurneys we meet him—attractive, mid-fifties, in blue scrubs. He also looks like he's been up all night.

"Mrs. Michelberg? I'm Dr. Ramberg."

"Call me Rachel, please." We shake hands and I introduce Paul.

"Do you want to sit down?" Apparently he's noticed my shaking legs, the lack of color in my face.

I glance at a gurney.

"It's OK," he says gently. "We can change the sheets."

Paul helps me up. My feet dangle awkwardly above the floor, like a three-year old on an adult-sized chair. Weird—but then the whole situation isn't exactly how I'd normally spend a Wednesday morning.

"I'm sure you already know how critical your husband's situation is, but we've stabilized him for now. In addition to the severe head trauma, David's pancreas has been badly damaged, and three vertebrae in his lower spine are shattered."

David won't walk again?

I look at Paul—all business, he's getting out a notepad. "Do you need to operate? Isn't that what you were just doing?"

"There's no internal bleeding at the moment, but we're keeping a close eye on the pancreas. We're not sure yet about the spine—we've induced a coma to immobilize him since he's on a respirator. But we'll make a decision in the next few days. Our primary concern is the skull and face injuries. And his brain, of course."

Paul lowers his notepad and takes a step closer. I feel his hand on the small of my back. "Where is David now?"

"In recovery. They'll bring him back to the ICU in the next hour or so. He'll be in a coma for several days. He'll need more surgeries, including facial reconstruction."

Elephant man.

Breathe. Use your yoga training. In through the nose, out through the mouth. My pounding heart fights that guidance. It's beating hard, filling my throat.

"David must have hit his head on the instrument panel. There's a large split in his skull from here"—Dr. Ramberg points to the bridge of his nose—"to here"—drawing a line to the crown of his head.

"Oh my God." I visualize an orange wedge sliced out of the giant red beach ball of David's face.

"We're worried about intracranial bleeding, so we removed skull fragments and inserted a cranial pressure monitor. It will keep us apprised of his brain activity. Or lack of activity."

Jesus Christ. Will he be a vegetable? Like Terry Schiavo, that poor woman who was brain-dead and on life support, comatose for over fifteen years, with her parents wanting to keep her alive at all costs, her husband fighting for her right to die. *Will there be a fight with David's family?*

"Often we have to relieve pressure from the swelling brain by drilling a hole in the skull. But David's skull is already cracked open, so we don't have to do that."

"Oh, haha, well that's good I guess." I laugh a little too loud. Paul and the doctor don't laugh. I can see myself, embarrassed.

"Come with me into the ICU. I'll show you the X-rays."

I'm not at all sure I want to see them. I force myself to nod my assent.

The ICU is humming, droning voices rising above the beeping of monitors. Day-shift nurses offer cautious smiles as we pass. Dr. Ramberg types something into a computer and David's crushed nose and forehead pop onto the screen. The fissure down the center of the skull is unmistakable.

"See this area here? This is the optic nerve. We're pretty sure it was deprived of blood flow. He will probably lose sight in that eye."

David with an eye patch. Like Ariel Sharon, or a pirate. *Aye, matey.* Or with the glossy staring look of the blind. "But the other eye is OK?" *Please, God.*

"We won't know until David is conscious and can answer questions. But we're doing everything we can."

Very reassuring. "Yes, of course you are. Thanks for everything."

The thundercloud of information isn't complete. There is a gaping hole, the unanswered question, the elephant. An enormous, aggressive beast with long tusks and massive stomping feet.

The doctor is leaving. I need to know. I open my mouth, but there is no sound.

Paul to the rescue. "What's the prognosis? Will David be in a vegetative state?"

Brain surgeons are—well, brain surgeons. Brilliant, but not particularly good at emotional perception. Dr. Ramberg surprises both of us by sitting down next to me.

"The fact that David has survived so far means that chances are good he will live." He pauses with a little frown. "The internal and spinal injuries will likely heal in time. But we don't know how much brain function he'll recover."

Uh oh.

"It actually could get worse before it gets better. His brain is continuing to swell and press against the skull, shearing off neurons. I know you don't want to hear this—but really, we just have to wait and see."

Waitandsee. I'm learning a new medical mantra. Will it bring me peace and enlightenment?

"In the meantime, hang in there and try to get as much rest as you can. I'll see you later." He gives me a tight-lipped smile. "David will be brought in shortly."

"Thanks," I mumble, trying to show my appreciation. Paul gives my shoulders a squeeze, and I gratefully accept his offer to fetch coffee for us. I turn back to the computer monitor, tracing my finger down the fissure on the screen. More surgeries to reconstruct his face.

What will my lawfully wedded husband look like? Not the attractive man I promised to stand by, in sickness and in health.

How shallow. Just be grateful he's alive.

Try to be grateful he's alive.

Commotion in the ICU. A gurney is pushed past me. I hold back a bit, waiting for the orderlies to transfer him ("On my count: one, two—three!") and hook him up to the machines surrounding his bed, a forest of ominously beeping trees.

I make my way to the bedside tentatively. There is one nurse left, checking monitors, the respirator, IVs, fluid levels. I'm afraid to touch him.

"He can't hear me, right?"

She smiles. "Not really, but you should talk to him anyway. We think it helps with the healing."

Healing? That seems like a pretty far-fetched idea. David looks about the same as he did last night, except the bloody bandages have been replaced with clean ones. Barely recognizable. So much swelling, so many tubes. Will it be months? Years? *Ever?*

Even if he survives, who will my husband be?

Who will I be?

My roles are clearly defined, and I do them pretty well. A mother and wife, yes, but mainly I think of myself as a professional classical and theater singer and a cantor. Pretty self-centered occupations, but you don't get leading opera roles baring your soul and talent in front of hundreds of people by focusing on others. You have to like attention—almost crave it. You have to spend countless hours practicing and rehearsing.

Although I always intended to have children, I had not prepared for the supreme selflessness parenting requires. Back-to-School Night? You have to miss rehearsal. You're sick and feel like crap? You still have to get out of bed, make the kids breakfast (and a bag lunch), and schlep them to school. You want those beautiful suede boots? You buy your daughter shoes instead, since she outgrows them every two minutes and buying both just isn't in the budget.

I resent my kids on occasion. Parenting is not a constant thrill. But I accept the role and forge ahead, constantly trying to find the balance, walking the tightrope between my needs and theirs. I'm learning to find joy in their accomplishments, not just in mine.

But I'm not a natural caretaker like David's mother Maria or his sister Dora. How can I possibly become David's nursemaid?

Especially now, when I'm falling out of love with him—and falling in love with Mark.

I stroke David's hand, trying to avoid the oxygen monitor on his index finger. His skin is dry, papery. *I should bring some of that nice lavender hand cream from home. Wait, he doesn't care. Hell, he may not even wake up.*

"Oh, David," I sigh, forcing myself to really study him. "Please don't die."

I say these words dutifully. But somewhere—in the most shameful, monstrous, depths of my being—I know I don't fully mean them.

Chapter 4

———————————————

PAUL AND I ROTATE BETWEEN THE ICU, the waiting room, the parking lot for a little fresh air, dispensing updates, and arranging logistics (thank God I remembered my phone charger). Miri leaves a voicemail—Yaron is still in the clinic in Paso Robles, in critical condition but lucid. He has a mild concussion but will need surgery to repair the vertebrae in his lower back. She'll call back with more news as it develops.

Paul takes on the unpleasant task of calling Mom, our Mistress of Worry. I'm in no mood to console her when I need so much consoling. I'm in no shape to handle more drama. My boss, Rabbi Dana, offers to send out email updates of David's condition so I don't have to repeat myself a million times. Lisa assures me that the kids are OK—she will probably take them to her house for a few days.

"Joshie's karate is today; Hannah has gymnastics on Thursday. The school is kosher, so don't send any ham in their lunchboxes. Hannah likes tuna, Joshie will only eat PB&J." What else does she need to know? "You can also reach out to Sue, Julie, Nora, and Karen," friends in the area who will be there to help, no questions asked. "Oh, and please go next door and ask Joe to feed the cat."

Joe and Mary are an older, childless couple who've lived in their little house for forty years, a proud part of the Italian community that had settled Willow Glen. Joe, who had been the postmaster at the local post office, is like a surrogate father to me and grandfather to the kids, offering gardening tips and lending tools—he has anything and everything we ever need. He loves to chat up our mail carrier at ten in the morning, tumbler of red wine in hand, Italian style. Mary makes the kids special Halloween treats. "Come inside," she'd beckon to Hannah in her Sleeping Beauty costume, Joshie as Tigger. "Shh. Don't tell the other kids."

We have a good community. We will have support.

David's older sister and brother are due to arrive in the early evening—Dora from Tel Aviv, Sigi from Munich. David has remained close to both of them despite how scattered they are—weekly phone calls, especially with Dora, have been de rigueur. Most of our pre- and post-kid vacations have been in Israel or Germany, and Dora and her youngest daughter, 11-year-old Michal, spent several weeks with us in California the past summer.

I'm especially fond of Dora. Funny, kind, upbeat, and seemingly tireless, she always has dinner on the table for her OB/GYN husband Rafi no matter how late he arrives home. Dora and I take long walks, chatting like old friends, connecting over my pregnancies (she was full of great advice: "Forget the doctor's warnings!" "Take that antacid for your heartburn, it won't hurt you!") and our husbands' dereliction of household duties. She complains about having to pick up one of her older teenage daughters from a Tel Aviv nightclub at three in the morning, but she keeps doing it every weekend anyway.

"Why doesn't she just say no?" I'd ask David. "When our kids are that age I'm going to draw the line. We can pick them up but it will have to be at a reasonable hour. Those girls run her life."

David rolled his eyes and shrugged. "That's Dora. Always taking care of everyone."

The oldest, Sigi, is sweet but more elusive. He isn't easy to nail down on commitment, be it a relationship, or making any kind of vacation plans with us.

"What does Uncle Sigi always say?" we teasingly prompt the kids.

"*Schauen wir mal!* We'll see!" they screech in delight.

Yet Sigi jumped on the first plane to California the moment he heard about the accident.

Paul and I are back in the ICU waiting room after a quick shower when they arrive. It's far from a happy reunion—grim greetings, anxious hugs. They are both haggard and drained from worry, long flights, and the drive from LAX. We give them a quick update and a warning about David's appearance. Dora's eyes fill with tears when she sees David lying motionless, just his chest rising with the force of the respirator filling his lungs. Sigi, normally jovial, is mute and ashen.

I reach for Dora's hand. For a while the four of us stand in silence except for the *beep beep, whoosh whoosh*.

―――――――

Our days fall into a kind of eerie routine—ICU, waiting room, parking lot, joyless meals in the hospital cafeteria. Paul goes home. We move into the motel, Sigi in one room, Dora and I sharing another. For lack of privacy, conversations with Mark are difficult. More than once I speak to him out on the balcony, telling Dora that I am talking to "a friend." Is she looking at me suspiciously, or is it my imagination?

Guilt pervades me. I have no business using Mark as support, but the idea of cutting him off is unimaginable. He's saying and doing all the right things. "You want me to stay away? I'll do whatever you need."

He brings up what I'm not able to verbalize. "Do you believe in divine intervention? Maybe David's accident is some kind of punishment from the Universe for our relationship." Nervous laughter. Then silence.

. — .—. — —.

The idea of *beshert*—that our very existence is determined by fate and some things are simply meant to be—seems ridiculous. A horrific tragedy has just befallen David, a good, decent man. A just God would be punishing me, a would-be adulterer. Perhaps I'm not quite a "sinner" yet, but I am indeed culpable. If David is being punished for my indiscretion, I'm not sure I can live with myself.

I choose not to go there.

David is to have plastic surgery the following day, *Erev Pesach*, Passover eve. On this Passover, instead of bowls of salt water and dishes of parsley and *charoset*, metal plates will be inserted into David's face to reshape his shattered cheekbones and forehead. This night will indeed be different from all other nights.

I make a few attempts with the local Jewish Community Center to find a Seder, but none of us are in the mood to eat gefilte fish and matzah with strangers. At least Hannah and Joshie will have Passover with my friend Nora's family. It has to be enough.

I am learning about survival mode. Get through the day, the hour. The next five minutes.

. — .—. — —.

I grow to love the nurses who patiently answer my barrage of questions. How long will he be here? Where will he go after this? Will he remember us? Will he be able to dress and feed himself?

The all-consuming question: If he doesn't return to normal, what will he be like?

The answer is always the same. We just don't know.

Schauen wir mal.

"Did you ever see *Regarding Henry?* With Harrison Ford?" one of my favorite nurses asks, re-hanging multiple IV drug bags, simultaneously checking and adjusting monitors.

I'm sitting on a chair at the foot of the bed, reading email. "No, but I heard about it."

She wipes some drool from David's chin. "Came out about ten years ago? So Harrison Ford is a real jerk, a lawyer I think. Super selfish and arrogant. Having an affair."

I look down at the screen. Ouch.

"Then he's involved in this robbery and gets shot in the head. He becomes a different person—compassionate and loving. All of his relationships get better."

Who is Harrison Ford kidding? Hollywood, please. I'm not that naïve. I study David's face and sigh. The swelling has gone down a little, the contours of his nose and cheeks emerge as if he's fighting to dig himself out of a hole, to clear away the muck that's buried him.

Suddenly I feel a rush of tenderness. I remember how David's pale grey-blue eyes grew moist as he looked down at me nursing Hannah for the first time. Running alongside Joshie's wobbly attempt at riding without training wheels. Making love after a day of skiing in Sun Valley, then giggling as we ran across the snow in our bare feet to sink into the steamy outdoor hot tub, grinning at each other as if we had a secret.

Who are you now, David? Who will you be? Will we ever share that secret grin again?

Will I be able to love you again?

Whoosh whoosh, beep beep.

When the cranial swelling goes down there will be a final surgery to close David's skull before they take him off of the respirator, possibly early next week. Dora and Sigi urge me to go home for a night or two to see the children. I miss them. Some clean underwear and fresh clothes would be nice, too.

Maybe I can sneak a few minutes to see Mark. *How fucked up is that?*

Lisa brings the kids home to meet me when I arrive late that Saturday afternoon. Hugging their little bodies close, I think about how drastically their young lives will be altered.

Essentially fatherless. Or worse: a shell as a father.

Joshie runs off to his room—video games await (I have no bandwidth to care about excessive screen time)—but Hannah fixes her wide brown eyes on me. "Is Daddy OK?"

Lisa and I had agreed that she would tell the kids that it was David who had been in an accident, not "a friend." But she was not to tell them just how serious it really is. That discussion will happen the next afternoon at Lisa's house. Rabbi Dana has offered to facilitate. The kids have a good relationship with him—Passover at his house, running around the sanctuary with Dana's son Raya during services.

But tomorrow is light years away.

I pull Hannah onto my lap and bury my face in her sweet-smelling hair, inhale deeply. "Oh honey, he's very sick. But the doctors are taking really good care of him."

I'm not exactly lying. Practicing the first of many gentle deceptions.

"Can you take me to see him?" She frowns, as if knowing the answer already.

"I'm afraid not. Children aren't allowed in that special area of the hospital."

"That's not fair!" She hops off my lap and glares at me accusingly. "Why not?"

"Because the people in that place are very, very sick. They need to stay quiet." She wasn't convinced. I searched for another reason. "Also, kids have germs they might give to the sick people and make them worse."

"Adults have germs, too."

"I know." I sighed. "It's not fair. I'll tell Daddy you said hi and that you hope he feels better soon."

I push away the memory of feeling ridiculous trying to talk to David in a coma. I don't really believe he hears anything. But if it helps Hannah to think David is getting the message—no brainer.

Hmmm. No brainer. Time to reconsider that phrase.

"OK. Tell him he has to get better so he can come see my gymnastics show."

My God, I love this little girl.

Her daddy won't make it to her show.

The doorbell rings. I hear Joshie scamper to the door. "Mommy, it's some guy with pizza," he yells.

"That's my friend Mark. He's brought us dinner. Isn't that sweet?" I'm shaking slightly as Mark follows Joshie into the kitchen, carrying two square boxes.

"Did you get pineapple?" Joshie is unsuccessfully trying to open one of the boxes.

"Slow down, buddy," I admonish. "Let me help you."

Mark, in David's kitchen, having takeout with David's kids. Awkward. *Whose brilliant idea was this? Oh right, mine.*

For a moment I wish he would get the hell out of my house. But as the kids run off to watch TV, slices on paper plates, Mark's hand cups mine when I hand him a glass of wine. Any thought of him leaving, of being out of my life, is unfathomable.

I'm desperate for normalcy, so we talk about the Anne Frank project we'd been planning. He'd written and received a grant for us to perform it in local elementary and middle schools in May. It would keep us joined, he'd said. Give us an excuse—an honorable excuse—to see each other.

"Do you want me to cancel it?" he asks, clearly not wanting to.

"Oh, no." I say, fiddling with my pizza crust, only able to choke down part of a small slice. "It's such an important project."

He gives me a look that says: is that really the reason?

I trace the palm of his hand under the table with my finger. That's not the real reason, says my touch.

I imagine him helping the kids get ready for bed, reading them a bedtime story, cuddling with me on the sofa. Afterward, making love to the transcendent harmonies of Brahms.

"Mommy, Hannah's watching *Zoey 101*, but it's my turn and I want *Drake and Josh!*" Joshie stomps into the kitchen. My little golden-haired boy, looking so much like David. Interrupting my reprehensible fantasy.

"No more TV. Go put your pajamas on, bud." I start clearing plates. "Hannah, pajamas!"

Mark picks up his cue. "I'd better go."

"I really appreciate you bringing dinner. Guys, can you say thank you?" I prompt, trying to give my best nonchalant impression of someone who didn't care that much.

"Thanks, bye," they both dutifully respond, running off to

start the bedtime routine. I walk Mark to the door, hugging my own arms. No more touching. At least not now.

"I'll call you soon," he promises.

I shake my head. "I'd better call you."

"Whatever you need." he smiles sadly, and is gone.

.—.—.—..

Rabbi Dana has to teach Sunday School the next morning so we meet in the early afternoon at Lisa's house. I'll drive back down to San Luis Obispo immediately afterward; the kids will stay at Lisa's. They aren't happy about it, understandably wanting to sleep in their own beds, surrounded by their toys, their books. But it works better for Lisa to have them at her home. I really can't protest, considering how much she's doing for me. For all of us.

"Let's sit over here," Dana says, motioning toward the living room where there are several comfy chairs and couches.

"Mommy," Hannah whispers, "why is the Rabbi here?"

"He has something he wants to talk to you and Joshie about." She looks alarmed. "Don't worry, honey. You're not in trouble."

Joshie plops onto a chair next to Ditto, their family Labradoodle, and tries to grab her beloved sock to throw. Ditto snatches it away each time before Joshie can get to it. This feels like a good distraction for the ominous news to come.

I'm fond of Lisa's cool-headed, witty husband Gordon, and glad he's with us. "I'll stand." He's already contacted some aviation law attorneys for me to interview.

"So you guys know that your dad was in an accident, right?" Dana asks.

"His plane crashed." Joshie has managed to procure Ditto's sock and is teasing her with it.

"Yeah, Aunt Lisa already told us." Hannah looks impatient. "But he's getting better."

"Well, your mom wanted me to explain about his injuries. He hit his head very hard when the plane crashed. It damaged his brain. The doctors aren't sure how much he'll recover." Dana goes on about head trauma, personality change, disabilities. Joshie doesn't seem to be registering much. He's abandoned the dog and is examining his Tamagotchi, an annoying electronic virtual pet that is all the rage.

Hannah moves closer to me, listening intently. She's gravely quiet. "Is Daddy going to die?"

The adults in the room seem to relax a bit with this query; she's getting it.

Dana pauses. "We don't know, sweetie. If he's made it this far, chances are he's not going to die. But for sure he's going to be very sick. He'll probably be in the hospital for a long time."

"Your dad is strong," Lisa says. "And the doctors and nurses are taking really good care of him."

Except for the clicking of Joshie dropping the Tamagotchi on the coffee table, it is quiet. Hannah is biting her lower lip with her familiar determined look—the look of trying not to cry. I smooth her hair, and she looks up at me.

"I guess Daddy can't come to my gymnastics show." She straightens up and clasps her hands together. "I think I can handle this."

Chapter 5

DAVID HAS JUST COME OUT OF surgery when I get back to San Luis Obispo and the ICU. Dora and Sigi report it has gone well. It's his last surgery for a while, though the doctors are still worried about his pancreas and the damaged vertebrae.

"When a patient is immobilized due to coma, the back will naturally start to heal. It's so much better than operating." How refreshing to hear a surgeon say that. "But we'll have to keep him immobilized long past the coma. We'll make him a torso brace to wear 24/7, for about ten weeks. It's like a big clamshell."

That sounds manageable. Uncomfortable for David, but manageable.

The ICU at Sierra Vista is outdated. The curtained "rooms" are mostly open, leaving patients pretty visible. I see some very grim people in the waiting room as I enter. I imagine they are relatives. Most of the other patients are elderly, but David has a new neighbor, twentyish. Dora shakes her head when I ask. "He's a construction worker, fell off a roof. I heard he's brain-dead."

The ICU is like a little tight-knit community, with an ever-changing cast of characters, complete with gossip and speculation.

We are standing by David's bed. I imagine my husband's brain: electrical impulses firing away, trying to find their way to link with neurons. Connecting well at the back but weakly or not at all at the front. Essentially a mangled motherboard. But nothing like David's neighbor, whose brain has virtually no activity of its own left. Its function will cease completely if the machines are turned off.

I wonder if it would have been better if David had not been kept alive. Again. But I give a silent prayer of thanks that I don't have to decide whether or not to remove him from life support.

David's coworker Dror is the first of several people to make the long drive to visit that week. By now I'm used to David's appearance, but Dror can't hide his shock. Do I also detect some guilt?

The four of us sit down for Styrofoam cups of coffee in the hospital cafeteria. Even Sigi, who doesn't like to leave David's side, is there. Dror has spent time with Yaron, the pilot, at the clinic in Paso Robles. "Everybody at Passavé feels horrible," he admits in his thick Hebrew accent, as if he is personally responsible. "We should have had regulations about flying. But you know, we're a startup, so we don't think about that stuff."

I glance at Dora, whose gaze is intent upon Dror. We've been waiting for what feels like an eternity to find out exactly what had happened that night.

Dror sips the watery coffee. "Yaron said it was a really beautiful evening for flying. But then they heard a loud bang and the—how do you say—the place where they were sitting?"

"Cockpit." Sigi says, before I can. I'm the only native English speaker at the table, but Sigi works for an airline.

"Yes, the cockpit filled with smoke. They contacted the tower and were told to fly toward an airport nearby. They headed there, but then the—the hood…" Dror makes a gesture of something opening with his hands. "I think it has a different name on an airplane?"

None of us can find the word. "Go on," Dora urges.

"The hood or whatever it's called flew up. They couldn't see anything."

"*Um Gottes willen.* Oh my God." Dora's breath locks up. Sigi grips his Styrofoam cup.

"Out of the side windows Yaron saw that they were flying toward some houses, so he veered away and headed toward what he thought was a field. But it turned out to be a vineyard."

I picture the beautiful rolling green countryside of the Central coast, wineries dotting the bucolic landscape. I had seen them from Highway 101 just the day before. It's so incongruous, that tragedy among grape vines.

My mind loop-d-loops. *Chardonnay? Petite Syrah?*

"They really thought they were going to land safely, so he lowered the landing gear. Just a few meters from the ground the gear caught in wire and those sticks holding up the vines . . ."

"Stakes," I murmur.

"*Ken.*" He uses the Hebrew word. "Yes, stakes."

"But I don't understand," says Sigi. "If they were so low to the ground how come David hit his head so hard? Weren't they wearing seatbelts?"

We look at Dror expectantly.

"Seatbelts, yes. But not shoulder harnesses. The plane didn't have them."

"Why not?" Dora demands.

"It was built in the '60s. Before they were required."

"It's called a grandfather clause.*" I explain. "Old models don't require retrofitting when the law changes."

Dror nods.

"Stupid clause," says Dora.

The next day marks a week since the accident. Our collective mood is slightly better with David scheduled to be taken off the respirator. He will remain heavily sedated until the clamshell is ready. There is a possibility that he'll be awake enough to speak.

My excitement dampens as soon as we arrive at the hospital. The ICU waiting room is filled with people I'd seen the previous day, ashen and somber relatives of the young man in the next bed. We're met at the door and asked to stay out of the waiting room by a serious-looking woman in her forties. His sister had told me they were going to wait a day, and then ask to have some of his organs harvested. That's what's happening.

Every four years I mark the little box on my driver's license. There's no question that it's the right thing to do. But reconciling that little checked box with the reality of this devastated family is jarring and humbling.

I almost envy them —at least they will have closure.

When the clamshell is ready, we are celebratory as we gather around David's bed, waiting for the removal of the breathing tubes. The respiratory therapist is poised, eyes glued to oxygen levels on the monitor.

---

*In 2005, the term "grandfather clause" was not commonly known to have racist origins. In this current (and long-overdue) environment of heightened awareness, I offer an opportunity to understand the racist origins of this practice which was one of the early tactics of voter suppression.

The doctor makes the proper adjustments to the ventilator equipment, slowly extracts the tubes that have been David's lifeline for over a week. David gags and jerks. Opens his eyes.

"He looks a little less like an alien now," I quip.

Everyone laughs. Laughter, scarce in my current world, is still alive.

"Do you know your name?" the doctor asks gently.

David clears his throat several times. Then in his high, reedy, German-accented voice, he says, "David." He clears his throat again. "David."

His voice is a surprise. Not that he is speaking—the doctors had said to expect that. Surprised that his voice sounds exactly the same. He sounds like my husband.

Perhaps I'd convinced myself that David wouldn't be David anymore, that everything—personality, appearance, behavior, even voice—would be altered completely. As a singer and voice specialist, I should have known better. His facial structure is indeed distorted, but his vocal folds aren't damaged.

David is still in there somewhere. Welcome back.

But I'm not sure who I'm welcoming.

Chapter 6

THERE IS PROGRESS. EACH DAY, EACH procedure, is closer to David's release.

David's discharge. A dark terrifying tunnel I am being forced into. A tunnel with no exit route. Will he be able to communicate? Be bedridden? Will I have to deal with a catheter? Change diapers? Feed and dress him? A baby in the house again?

Will I have to have sex with him?

And the kids. How will they handle an invalid father? Will their friends be afraid to come for play dates—repulsed by David's appearance, his behavior?

I imagine Hannah and Joshie embarrassed by their father. As teens that's to be expected, but not at six and seven.

Perhaps most frightening—I won't see Mark (at least not easily) when David is home. And he'll be home all the time. All. The. Time. In our little house. With me.

I mull these questions. No way to share my horrifying fantasies with Dora or Sigi. Especially the one about Mark. David is their baby brother. I have no thought of abandoning my obligations as David's wife.

Maybe the vows need to be amended, adding, "except if I'm going to have a mental breakdown."

I don't believe David will be coming home. At least not right away. He's in critical condition.

My priority is to find him a hospital with a good head injury department. It is pure luck that Santa Clara Valley Medical Center, our local county hospital renowned for its trauma center, is just a few miles from our house. It's news to me that county hospitals often specialize in trauma, but they regularly treat uninsured patients who indulge in reckless behavior. Their brain injury unit is typically filled with un-helmeted motorcycle riders.

They don't need to plan for plane crashes. Most people don't survive.

Plans are finalized for David to be transported by helicopter to the ICU on Friday. Sigi has to return to Munich for job and family. Dora wants to stay on. I'm relieved. She will tag-team with me at the hospital, help with the kids, and be good company. She wants to take care of all of us. But how will I see Mark?

I need Dora more than him.

As we drive up Highway 101, Dora points. "Look, there's the helicopter." We watch it fly past, a tiny dot in the bright sky over the hilly, green central coast.

David is finally flying home.

Our time in San Luis Obispo has been like a tragic play, the hospital and motel room the stage set. Back in San Jose, driving on streets I use to take the kids to school and buy groceries—rejoining these daily routines is way too close to reality. A good wife, an honorable person, would be thrilled that David has progressed enough to be moved, even if he is going straight into another hospital. Wouldn't she?

But I'm just thanking God he isn't coming home. For now.

. —.—.— —.

David is in the ICU for another few days, then transferred to the regular medical floor while the pancreas is healing. A medical army is assigned: a physiatrist to oversee his rehab, a psychiatrist, an internist, an orthopedist. Later the regiment will include an ophthalmologist and a whole battery of therapists: speech, occupational, and physical. Keeping track of everyone and all of David's treatments will become my full-time job.

Meals are brought to our house, arranged by our Jewish community. I'm grateful, but I can barely choke anything down. The kids love the meals that arrive—chicken nuggets, plastic containers of Safeway cookies, fruit roll-ups ("as a special treat," reads a sticky note). Nutritional concerns for the kids? I have no bandwidth to care.

Nor am I ready for them to visit David. He isn't exactly Elephant Man anymore, but his face is unfamiliar. A little scary. The crevasses make him look craggy, angular. He's lost a ton of weight, his head is shaved. Like a concentration camp survivor.

Like his father Samuel who survived Auschwitz.

In truth, it isn't his appearance I'm afraid for the kids to see. It's the man who isn't really their father anymore. A man whose one functioning eye will probably never again see them the familiar way, the way a normal father sees his kids. Pride, anger, protectiveness—none of it will be as it had been.

Though I'm not ready, I take them. Hannah is anxious. Joshie bounces off the walls, over-stimulated. He keeps trying to get on David's bed to touch his face. I'm fine with that—at least he isn't fearful.

David, however, is annoyed. "Get that boy off me."

Intrigued by the numbers on the heart monitor, Joshie doesn't hear. Luckily. But Hannah does.

"Daddy, that's Joshie." She's confused, though Dora and I have tried to prepare her.

David gazes at her, the fissure in his forehead deepening. "Why is Keren here? Isn't she in Germany?"

Keren, Dora's eldest daughter, is in the Israeli army.

Hannah's lower lip quivers. I take her small hands and gently place them on David's. "Hannah is seven, David. She's our daughter. Remember?"

He wants to, I can see.

But he doesn't.

This is our new normal.

· — ·— · — · ·

Among friends and work colleagues, David is as popular here as he was in Germany. He loved socializing, regularly organizing Vietnamese lunches, billiards, drinks, paintball. My women friends complain about having to play the social secretary in their marriages. David has always had lots of male friends and never waited for me to make plans. I liked that about him.

Once he is allowed visitors it's no surprise that most of his friends come to see him. No one knows what to say. David masters a few words, sometimes rambling nonsense. Although he pretends to, he often doesn't know who they are. His friends end up talking mainly with me.

Dr. Malcolm Lawton stops by. "Hello, Rachel. Hi, David."

David gives a bright smile, but there is no recognition in his eyes.

"Oh, Dr. Lawton. Hi." I am always happy to see doctors, no matter the reason—someone who can shed some light on the situation, someone who might offer a glimmer of hope.

"This is Venkat and Rob. They used to work with David at AMD."

Strained smiles all around. Nobody wants to be here. It's what you do when your critically injured friend is in the hospital—you come, offer help, maybe call a few times, show you care. Then usually, unintentionally, you fade away.

Dr. Lawton gestures to the hallway. "Rachel, may I speak with you outside for a minute?"

I look at the guys.

"No problem," Rob turns and says, "David, how's the food in this place?"

"Not bad," I hear David's words as I make my way out of the room. "I had filet mignon last night."

Filet mignon? At the county hospital? Either David is his old teasing self or he is confabulating—making up responses—because despite the massive injuries, he knows he is expected to give an answer. I guess the latter.

There isn't usually a place to sit in hospital hallways, so I lean against a wall.

"Do you want to go to the terrace?" Dr. Lawton asks. "We can sit down."

"No, no, I'm fine. You probably don't have much time."

The doctor fixes his eyes on me. "How are *you* doing?" Emphasis on the "you," as if to say, *This isn't all about David. I know how hard this is for you.*

Dr. Lawton isn't officially his doctor, but as a member of David's synagogue he heard about the accident and offered his support. Malcolm Lawton is grandfatherly, short and slight, like he might fall over in a strong wind. But he works with brain injured people all day long in outpatient rehab. David might be his patient one day. I'm beginning to understand how strong, how heroic these medical people are—especially those who work in rehab—when results can take months or years to attain. Their patience is unfathomable. Patience I don't have.

"I'm OK."

One glance tells me Dr. Lawton knows that answer is horse-shit. It seems that this guy really wants to know.

"Actually, I'm a mess." Tears well up. "Obviously," I mumble.

He fishes a tissue out of his pocket and, with sympathetic eyes, offers it to me.

I blow my nose and wad the tissue tightly in my hand. How many of these will I use before this is over? Will I ever stop crying? I should buy stock in Kleenex.

I'm not at all sure I really want to know, but I have a feeling this man won't sugarcoat it. "Please can you tell me the truth?" I stare at the tissue. I can't look him in the eye. "What will happen to David? Will he recover? Will I get my husband back? No song and dance please."

Dr. Lawton shifts his weight, appearing to contemplate my request. He chews his lower lip.

"No Rachel, I'm afraid not."

I knew it. I'd known it from the first moment I saw David after the accident.

Dr. Lawton clears his throat. "He'll never be the same. Not even close. The damage was so extensive, it's not remotely conceivable that he could recover enough to work. Or to live independently. He might improve, but only slightly. And even that's not a given. The brain doesn't regenerate like other organs—and David's brain is seriously messed up."

Finally. Someone is telling me the truth. Confirming the truth I already knew.

"When his back heals he'll be able to walk. As you know, he can talk and swallow—functions that are controlled by the back of the brain, the brain stem. But David's frontal lobes were really smashed up. The part that controls speech, memory, movement. Personality. He could also have trouble with toileting. Often TBI—traumatic brain injury—patients don't pick up their bodies' cues."

Dr. Lawton gives me a moment to register this prophecy.

"He'll probably be very impulsive," he continued, "without much ability to filter. Like a child."

I picture David in a diaper throwing a tantrum in the cereal aisle at Safeway. "I'll have a giant toddler on my hands?"

"At first, yes. It may improve later, but not by that much. He'll probably never get past the mental capacity of a seven-year-old."

Hannah's age. But Hannah will grow up.

Tears flow, dripping down my cheeks and onto my T-shirt. It's more release than fresh sorrow. I finally have a candid glimpse into the future. The other doctors hadn't exactly lied, but indirectly hinted at the possibility—remote though it is—of David working, being a father to our kids, playing pool with his friends. Becoming a new and improved David, like Harrison Ford.

"You need another Kleenex—I'll be right back." Dr. Lawton heads to the nurses' station. He is probably glad for an excuse to escape.

I wipe my nose on the back of my hand and gaze up at the fluorescent lights that line the hallway. Harsh, unforgiving light. Why can't they make hospitals softer?

"Here." Dr. Lawton holds out a fresh tissue. His eyes are sympathetic. "I'm just so sorry."

"Thank you," I manage to murmur. I take his hand. "Thank you for being honest."

He shakes his head slightly to acknowledge my need to be told the truth with this kind of candor.

These are facts. *Now* what do I do?

Chapter 7

HANNAH'S SCHOOL JOURNAL—MAY 2, 2005

A couple weeks ago, my dad had a plane crash. This is how it happened:

My dad was supposed to go on a business trip for 1 day, but when he came back he crashed. He broke many bones and had to have sergury. When my mom herd about it, she had to rush to get things ready. When it was time to say goodbye, my mom didn't really give us a kiss. For the rest of the time, I didn't get to see my dad.

"Aren't you going to finish that?" Julie asks.

My friend sits with me at a tacky coffee shop across the street from the hospital. She isn't the only one who notices that I'm getting very thin. I've forced down half of my sandwich, am poking at the other.

"No, I'm not really hungry."

She nods. Compassion is clear on her face. "Take it home—you can have it later. You need to take care of yourself."

What I don't tell her is that I'd stopped eating normally months before David's accident. Guilt about Mark had bred an appetite-killing parasite that inhabited my belly and brain.

Still carrying some of that pregnancy fat, eh Rachel? He might see you naked. You don't really want to eat that, do you? Get skinnier! You can do it!

These thoughts are familiar. If the affair was the catalyst, the crash was the full gas tank, the charged-up battery for an old eating disorder. I needed control in an uncontrollable situation.

- - - - - - -

The summer after sophomore year in college—1981—I was waitressing at Houlihan's, a hip restaurant frequented by aspiring Silicon Valley techies. I had my eye on playing one of Tevye's daughters—preferably Hodel, who has the good song—at a local community theater production of *Fiddler on the Roof.* Subconsciously, my main goal that summer was getting my weight down to two digits.

In a photo from that spring, I'm wearing a beloved cream-colored blouse with my arm around my mom. I have light brown hair, stylishly cut and meticulously blown dry in a long shag, frizzy and brittle like the "before" shot in a bad shampoo commercial. Oversized blue plastic glasses—'80s early chic—dwarf my sharp cheekbones, obliterate my angular, pinched face. The sticks exposed by the short sleeves of my rayon blouse can't possibly be my arms. Even sadder than my arms is Mom's expression. Her lips are curved in a heroic attempt to smile, but there's nothing joyous in her face. Rather it's the tight, desperate gaze of a mother whose baby is dying while she feels powerless to stop the withering.

At the time, Mom said I looked like a well-dressed concentration camp survivor. She was hoping to convince me to eat again.

It didn't work.

I was willingly in therapy. Dr. Stan Fishman was a sweet, middle-aged psychiatrist who specialized in eating disorders. Ironically, he was a bit overweight. We'd had several chats about opera (which he loved) and Judaism (he was Conservative and kept kosher.)

"El Camino hospital has a program. You'd stay there until you reach a healthy weight. No forced feeding. You'd be in control. Rewards if you gain, restrictions if you maintain or lose. I'll come to talk with you every day."

Ignoring Mom's hopeful looks (she sat in on a few sessions), I actually laughed. "Are you kidding? I have too much to do. My new job, and the show."

I knew my dying was killing Mom, too, but I refused.

At Houlihan's, we wore multi-colored maxi skirts and bright red clingy T-shirts that made me feel self-conscious about my D-cup breasts—very un-trendy during the Jane Fonda "feel the burn'"70s and early '80s—but I was proud of my flattening chest and newly boyish hips. My trophy: a testament to perseverance, discipline, control. I was winning. I was strong, brave, accomplished, noble. I was becoming an expert at suffering.

I darted around the restaurant during that training week like a long-legged shore bird hopping on the beach looking for insects. Obediently, I shadowed the experienced wait staff, compelling myself to remember the cooks' names, what types of salad dressings we offered, and where the extra sugar packets were stored. At the end of the week we would be tested on the menu—which didn't worry me. By then I'd performed leading roles in several musicals and an Italian opera. None of those other wannabe waitresses could put *that* on their resume. Memorization? Bring it on.

There was only one problem. I was always hungry. Always.

And everywhere there was food. Food to smell, order, keep track of, organize, study, carry, clean—anything and everything, except to eat. After each shift, the employees got a free meal—usually something fried and/or sauce-laden and ridiculously caloric. Greedily, I inhaled the fumes, only allowing a morsel or two (when I was being really sinful) onto my plate. I had become skilled at dissection. While everyone else was wolfing down the free lunch, I studied my solitary chicken strip, carefully removing the breading and methodically cutting it into pieces no bigger than a kernel of corn. I pushed those around the plate to draw out the meal as long as possible. I downed diet soda and sucked on lemon wedges in a vain attempt to fill my empty belly.

I remained hungry.

Apparently everyone else was getting sick of hearing me constantly talk about food. That Friday, after the final training shift was over and we'd all taken the menu test (how do you make a Shamrock Shake? What kind of cheese is on the Clover Cobb Salad?), I was asked to meet the assistant manager in her office, where she politely, but firmly, fired me.

"We think you might have an eating disorder," she said gently. "You seem pretty focused on food, and you are awfully thin. We will pay you for this week and give you another weeks' wages."

Her smile was sad. I was getting used to seeing smiles like that.

"Also, you didn't do very well on the menu test."

What the hell? No way! I'm a great student. I studied that stupid fucking menu. My GPA is 3.86. Who the hell does she think she is? OK, maybe it was a little hard to concentrate this week with all that food everywhere.

She stood up, indicating that the meeting was over. "Go home and get well, Rachel. Feel free to apply again when you're healthier."

I couldn't even be pissed off. She was maddeningly nice for someone who had just utterly humiliated me.

I don't know how I made it home. If she had pronounced a diagnosis of terminal cancer, I couldn't have been more stunned. I was a failure. I'd never failed at anything before. A moment before my life was perfect—I was young, pretty, talented, smart, and skinny and getting skinnier. I was the good girl who got every job I wanted and always got the solo, played the lead.

My hands shook on the wheel of my little green '72 Pontiac. My heart was hammering and I was breathing hard, as if I was about to go onstage to sing a high C in front of the casting director of the Metropolitan Opera. It was 2:30 on a beautiful Friday afternoon in June—but I had nowhere to go. I had no job, no shows, no friends nearby. I was going home to my father's condo—where his new wife didn't want me. The summer stretched out in front of me like the Donner Party facing the Great Salt Desert—long, dry, and hungry.

Hiking up my now-hated maxi skirt, I trudged up the shag-carpeted stairs to the ugly, institutional box of a room where I was camping out until school started again in the fall. Nothing hung on the walls except a badly framed poster of Monet's water lilies. I lay on the hard mattress, dry-eyed, staring at the popcorn ceiling. The emptiness I'd been proudly identifying as a shrinking stomach now felt like one of those flesh-eating bacteria, eating at me from the inside, reaching its tentacles to my toes, fingertips, even the dry split ends of my hair.

I can't even keep a fucking waitress job. I'm a worthless failure. I have no purpose. I have no value. I have no reason to live.

I'm pretty sure I don't believe in God. But if She exists, She spoke to me then.

"Yes, you do," She said. "Do Fishman's program. Check yourself into the hospital."

I sat up in bed and picked up the phone. "Mom?" I whispered. "I'm ready."

. —.—.— —.

Twenty-four years later, there is no Dr. Fishman. No special eating disorder support group for middle-aged, adulterous wives of TBI patients. But I'm not paying attention to the anorexia. I don't have time, let alone energy. I'm busy surviving each day.

David is moved to the head trauma inpatient rehab unit for regular occupational, physical, and speech therapy. His roommate Robert's bed is encased in a tent-like covering attached at the bedrails. "He can be aggressive," explains the occupational therapist.

Great. Just great.

"Don't worry, David will be safe. Robert can't figure out how to undo the attachments."

. —.—.— —.

HANNAH'S SCHOOL JOURNAL—MAY 11, 2005
I saw my dad two times. He is getting a lot better. I can't wait to see him again. I get to go once a day. My mom took a picture of him, and when I saw it, I cried a little. But I am very happy. I am happy because my dad is in a wheelchair today! I can't wait to roll him around the hospital. Every day is fun with Daddy.

. —.—.— —.

After four weeks Dora needs to go back to Israel. She plans to join us again when David comes home. We still have no idea when that will be.

"I'll definitely come back sometime this summer." She is always reassuring.

I'll miss her, though she's protected me from sliding further down my wayward path. Mark and I've managed some furtive phone calls, a few coffees, more than a few kisses. He is all I have that is hopeful—however illusory. My prince charming, with an intact brain.

"What's going to happen with us?" I murmur into Mark's neck as we hold each other on my living room sofa. It still smells of cat piss. "How will I see you when David's here all the time?"

There's been talk of hiring someone when he's home, a day-care provider to free me up a little. I hold Mark more tightly. The image of David, the kids, a caretaker, and the cat bashing into each other in our tiny house makes me:

- feel like throwing up.
- want to scream.
- think that all the chardonnay in the world can't calm my terror.
- believe my life is over.
- seriously concerned for my sanity.

"I don't know," Mark presses his lips to my hair. "I wish I had an answer."

If it weren't time to pick up the kids from school, I'd lead him by the hand into the bedroom I had shared with David. I hadn't wanted my first time making love with Mark to be born from desperation—but I don't care anymore. My fantasies of a perfect, beautiful, romantic adventure seem pathetic. All I want to do at that moment is fuck. As if it might be my last time.

I get in the car.

- — -— - — -·

Hannah continues piano lessons and gymnastics; Joshie is doing karate. I bring them to visit David several times a week. A sense of normalcy becomes my goal. Meals keep arriving, though I reduce them to twice a week. I'm barely eating.

A massive white board in the head trauma rehab unit displays a schedule of therapies for each patient. David has only two to three hours on weekdays. Weekends, nothing. I am dismayed. David is stuck in his room with tented Robert, immobilized in the clamshell. Would he watch *The Price Is Right* or *General Hospital* all day? I stare at the board, feeling guilty for not wanting to keep him company, to keep him occupied. I know I'm projecting my own fear of boredom—David has always been fine with unstructured time. He perceives the passage of time differently now that his brain is screwed up.

But Jewish genes are powerful little devils. Guilt—that useless, pesky emotion—supersedes rationality. Even when I don't bring the kids, I try to come every day, especially when I know he won't have other visitors.

It's the right thing to do.

· — ·— · — ·· —

The speech therapist lays five cards on the table. "David, these are household objects. Can you tell me which one is the fork?"

David points to a card.

"Good," she said. "And what do you use it for?"

He studies the ceiling. I can tell he can't find the word, can't make the connection between the item and its use.

"Cutting food."

The therapist isn't daunted. She mimes eating with a fork. "Can you try again?"

"Eating."

"Exactly." She finds a picture of a knife in her pile. "What is the word for this object? This is the one that's used for cutting."

David looks at the ceiling again.

"Let me help you. It starts with a 'k.' It's a silent letter."

"English isn't David's mother tongue," I offer. "Spelling is hard, even before the accident."

David mutters something under his breath and leans back in his chair.

"You seem upset. Are you angry?" the therapist asks.

"I'm right here. You talk about me like I'm not here."

I sigh. Will I ever get this right? "I'm sorry, David. I'm trying to help, but that was wrong of me."

After the session we make our way back to the room. The therapist pulls me aside. "Anger is good—better than passivity for cognitive healing. Pride shows a sense of self. It may get worse before it gets better."

How can it get worse?

. —.—. — . .

The care team decides it's time for David to come home. He's been at Valley Med for three weeks and is medically stabilized, though still in the clamshell. The date is set for the Saturday before Memorial Day.

D-day. Inevitable. *Deal with it.*

None of the logistical details have been worked out. Will I drive him to outpatient rehab, or would he be picked up by one of those white Outreach vans? Will I have to help him shower, use the toilet? David has lost a lot of weight, but I can't hold him up alone, especially in my own frail state. The clamshell is a pain in the ass to manage. David's demeanor is mostly passive, but what if he starts getting aggressive, like Robert? Will I have to protect the kids from their father? Is there a hotline for TBI spouses like there is for battered women? I imagine my frantic call: *Help—I'm afraid for my children's safety. I'm afraid for my sanity.*

"You'll get support," Lois, the social worker from the workers' comp insurance, sounds confident in her assurance. She is my guardian angel, a petite feisty brunette with a penchant for tailored jackets and low-heeled pumps. I want to crawl into her arms. "If you can have family and friends there for the first few days, we'll arrange for a regular caregiver to come during the day to give you a break."

Even in my numb state it's clear a few hours will not be enough. But I go along with the plan, amorphous as it is. I don't have the strength to think past that day, nor the next hour. I am becoming a survival mode expert.

Anyway, there are no options.

The morning before D-day I pick up food for the welcome home barbecue I'd arranged for Sunday. *What the fuck was I thinking?* I scold myself as I race through the aisles at Costco tossing hummus, carrots, packages of chicken and chips into the cart. *Just what I need. More on my plate.*

But I know exactly why I'd planned this gathering. I'm postponing being alone with David. The days of filling time, planning activities, loom before me like an ominous cloud.

I unload the groceries at home and rush to Valley Med for a quick meeting with Lois and David's rehab doctor to finalize the details of the transition. There will be another appointment back at the hospital later that afternoon with the ophthalmologist to find out if David's blindness is permanent. Though I've already been told it would be, this is to be the official prognosis.

Mark's Lexus is parked in front of the house when I arrive.

Is there any doubt we should have sex? Our lovemaking feels obligatory. *Now or never. My last chance.* It's disappointing, dutiful. There is no afterglow, no basking in pleasure. We lie together for a while. Awkward. Uncomfortable conversation periodically fills the space.

I catch the clock: 2:30. "Shit, David's eye appointment. I have to go."

We kiss goodbye. I feel removed, a transparent barrier between us. Have I already moved on? I hope so.

"I'll call you soon," he says. And I know that that call is still my life preserver. It can't be over. Not yet.

Sprinting down the hospital corridor, I see David sitting in his wheelchair waiting for me, unaware of how late I am. With each step I feel the familiar post-coital soreness after a long abstinence, usually a pleasant reliving of a passionate encounter, now just shame. I almost wish David would confront me, scream with anger at my betrayal, selfishness, neediness. Wake me to the reality of this new life: wheelchairs, doctors, helplessness. *Stop feeling sorry for yourself, you bitch. Look at* me. *I'm the one whose life has been fucked up.*

He gazes at me blankly.

"Come on, David, let's go." I release the brakes on the wheelchair.

"Are you my wife?"

One would expect me to be hurt, or surprised at the very least. "Yes, I'm Rachel. We're going to the eye doctor." As we pass, I wave to the nurses at the station. I press the elevator button. "I'm hoping they're going to tell us that your good eye will still be OK."

Because the alternative is unthinkable.

David's seeing eye will indeed be fine. He'll need to wear protective glasses as a precaution. For the rest of his life. And avoid sports.

"I'm pretty sure he won't be trying out for the NBA, right, David?" I quip. As if David can comprehend sarcasm. He doesn't even look confused. Anything said on any kind of deeper level, especially humor, flies right over his head. A category of loss that hasn't even occurred to me.

A wave of sadness verges on pity. It seems unfair that he has to look up at me, so I crouch next to David's chair in the darkness of the eye exam room.

"We're going to get through this, David." I squeeze his hand. "You still have a good eye. You're coming home tomorrow. You'll have more time with the kids."

But I'm on the wrong side. He has to turn his head to see me.

"What kids?"

· ─ ·─ ·─ · ─ ─·

The pain starts that night while I'm fixing dinner. Sharp, stabbing, lower left side. Within a half hour, every step is agony. I know exactly what it is— I've had several episodes. Diverticulitis—an excruciating inflammation in pockets of the large intestine.

Shit. Could my situation get any worse? Apparently yes.

"Joshie didn't bring his plate to the sink," Hannah complains, mouth full of volunteer-provided lasagna. Through the kitchen window I can see Joshie already across the street, going to play with the neighbor kid.

"*I'm* the mommy. That's not your business," I remind her for the millionth time, wincing in pain as I walk over to pick up his dish. It would have been more effort to get him back to the kitchen. Another good parenting opportunity squandered. "Nobody likes a tattler."

"What's wrong?" Hannah stops eating and stares at me, hunched over in a chair, clutching my belly.

"I'm not feeling very well, honey." God, it takes so much effort, hiding this pain.

The look on her face screams: *You can't be sick, Daddy's the sick one. Who will take care of us? We only have one parent now. Don't leave me.*

"Can you bring me my phone? I'm going to call the doctor. He'll give me some medicine, and I'll feel better." With great effort I open my arms, and she presses herself against me. I take her face in my hands and lock my brown eyes with hers. "I'll be OK, honey. I promise. Now go get my phone, please?"

I know exactly what will be prescribed, a nasty cocktail of two potent antibiotics that produce a horrible metallic taste in my mouth and a nauseous, generally crappy feeling. Worse, I can't drink alcohol during the course of the drugs. Facing David's homecoming without even a little chardonnay for solace is turning this normally uncomfortable and unfortunate illness into a disaster.

D-day. I can barely drag myself out of bed to make the kids breakfast. Though it's a Saturday, I call Lois. She assures me that she will arrange for David to stay at Valley Med until I feel well enough to bring him home. I should be grateful. Instead I feel like I'm cheating, postponing the inevitable. I want to get it over with.

With my guilt meter already in the red zone, I avoid telling Lois about the next days' party. With the antibiotics, usually the pain diminishes after a day or two. I will soldier on. David will get his party, if it kills me. And it might.

Sunday I'm in agony on the sofa, cat piss and barbecue smells intensifying my nausea. Friends and family who have rallied to help—transporting David, cooking and setting out food, come in periodically to check on me and bring me food that I can't eat.

The party is in full swing in the backyard—much to my dismay I can hear the Backstreet Boys. Hannah must have chosen the music. Oh well. It's not my party anyway. It's David's.

"You're not supposed to take these pills on an empty stomach," my friend Karen admonishes, examining the bottles.

"I know, but I feel like throwing up," I reach for the bowl on the floor and puke.

She brings a washcloth. We both see the undigested pills in the bowl.

"You need to eat something. Let me bring you some milk or yogurt with the next dose. Do you think you can get that down?"

I can't.

Early the next morning, after a miserable night, I call my internist who insists I go to the emergency room. Immediately. Dr. Dave is my age, a member of our congregation. Hannah and his son Joey are in school together. He'll meet me there.

I call Karen to take the kids to school and Lisa to drive me to the ER at O'Connor Hospital. She tries to distract me as I prepare for a contrast CT scan by drinking several large containers of a nasty-tasting concoction. It's a herculean effort to show interest as she rattles off newsy stories about her sons.

Dr. Dave is there when the CT results come back. He is grim. "You have a perforated colon. Normally it's a life-threatening condition but because you were able to keep some of the antibiotics down, the perforation's walled off. It's still serious—the tiny hole has allowed toxic waste to dump into your bloodstream. You're lucky you don't need a colostomy bag," he frowns. "Actually, you're lucky to be alive."

My definition of luck is changing by the minute.

"I'm going to admit you—they'll administer the antibiotics intravenously." Dave is gentle. "You'll need at least a nine-day course—usually it's ten, but you kept some of them down over the weekend."

My good-girl mind is screaming. *No fucking way! I can't stay here. Hannah will freak out. Joshie will be so confused. They've been through too much already. And David will be stuck at Valley Med for another nine days? No!*

"You need a break from what's happening." Dave puts a hand on my blanket-covered knee. "Let the nurses take care of you."

I see him exchange looks with Lisa. *The stress is too much for her*, the look says. *She's losing it.*

I close my eyes against the tears and lie back on the hard gurney. I'm nineteen again, ninety-seven pounds, lying on the bed in my father's condo, staring at the desert. No way to go but forward, but no strength to start the journey. I have to let go, let others carry me. For now, at least.

I open my eyes. "I'm ready."

Chapter 8

HANNAH'S SCHOOL JOURNAL ENTRY—
MAY 26, 2005

This is a really great week and sort of a bad week. The good thing is that my dad will come home this weekend! I have been waiting for him to come home for one month. But on Sunday, he came home for a couple hours. But this is better because he will be home forever. My mom will just love it when he gets home. But he will not go to work for almost one year. While he is not at work he will be at physical therepists. The bad news is that my mom is in the hospital too. She is in the hospital because on Saturday, May 21, my mom had pain. Then on Monday she went to the emergeny room and got a catscan. They said they have to stick a needle in her blood vain and they said it would take a couple days. On Monday, May 23, I got sick. I missed the end of year night at school. So that is the story of having a good week and sort of a bad week.

"The new admit in 524 is really fragile. May have an eating disorder. Also something about her husband at Valley Med with a recent TBI. And she has young kids." *The nurses don't seem to realize I can hear them perfectly. Oh well, it's good they're aware that I'm a mess.* I want them to appreciate how miserable I am. Maybe I'll get extra attention.

"Your doctor requested this room—you're getting special treatment." She is swabbing my inner arm for the IV. "It's normally reserved for cancer patients on palliative care."

I examine my home for the next nine days. Spacious, with a big window. A small pastel sofa, bland paintings. And the best part—no roommate. I say a silent prayer of thanks to Dr. Dave.

Lisa has made arrangements for childcare—my mother is taking the first shift and will bring the kids later that day. Joshie will be blissfully ignorant of the implications of my illness. But both Hannah and Mom will need support—a lot of reassurance that I'm not going to die.

"Mommy!" Joshie shrieks, running in ahead of his sister and grandmother. "Eee-yuuu. Why is that needle in your arm? Does it hurt?"

"Joshie, don't touch that," scolds Hannah.

I don't reprimand her for being bossy. I pull a blanket over the IV site. I wish I'd asked them to cover it.

"It's Mommy's medicine," my mother says. "She needs it to get well."

Mom pulls up a chair next to the bed, sits down and sighs. Picking up the kids from school is stressful for her. Since her treatment and miraculous survival of pancreatic cancer four years earlier, she's easily stressed. I show Joshie the buttons to raise and lower the bed.

"Thanks for doing the pickup, Mom."

"Oh honey, it's OK. I wish I could do more for you." She pulls Hannah onto her lap. "Mommy's going to be fine."

"Grandma said you had to be here for nine days." Hannah is reproachful. "That's a really long time. I thought Daddy was coming home, but now you're both gone."

"I know, sweetie, it's sad. But we all have to be strong."

"I get to go to Eitan's house for a sleepover!" Joshie announces. *God bless Lisa for making childcare arrangements.* "That's great, bud. You'll have fun."

"Grandma, don't squeeze so hard." Hannah wriggles to get out of her grasp. Mom is struggling not to cry.

"Come here," I say. "You're kind of heavy for Grandma Judy."

Hannah climbs onto the bed and I take her in my arms, careful of the IV.

I look over her head at Mom. "We'll get through this. What did you tell me recently? 'When you're walking through hell, just keep walking.'"

Mom pulls a Kleenex from the box on the meal tray and blows her nose. "I like that. I wish I'd thought it up."

I laugh. I haven't forgotten how. It feels great. "Do you know where it's from? You told me once that most great quotes came from either Shakespeare or the Bible."

"Pretty sure it's not from either of those places." Mom smiles. "But it's a good one."

----- -- --

I'm not permitted food by mouth, but a steady stream of well-meaning visitors bring smoothies along with requested magazines and books. Mark tries to time his visit to avoid encountering anyone. Unsuccessfully. A member of my choir from the temple is there when he arrives.

"You remember Mark, our musician from Yom Kippur?" I stammer.

Yes, of course she remembers him. We both heave a small sigh of relief when she leaves.

"You look great," he says, safe at the foot of my bed, squeezing my toes through the sheet.

"Liar." I try fluffing my hair, flattened by grease. Useless. "I look like crap."

"OK, you've had better days, but it could be a lot worse."

"I could have a brain injury?"

"What? Oh, um, yeah, that would be worse."

Awkward.

"You like strawberry banana? I didn't know what to get." He nods at the smoothie he's left on the table.

"Love it," I shake my head ruefully, "but nothing by mouth. I'm supposed to be fed through the IV at some point. It's going to be a super fun nine days."

He strokes his mustache. "I can't say I've ever put anyone in the hospital after having sex with them."

"Yeah, well, lucky me."

We avoid voicing our thoughts: *Is my illness part of the punishment for crossing the line? Karma biting us in the butt?* My mind adds: *So why is Mark getting off so easy?*

- --- - -- - -

Everyone is kind. My favorite nurses are the nuns who usually take the night shift. They don't wear habits, but their nametags say "Sister so and so, RN."

During the day I'm able to hold it together, mostly. But the long nights—the quiet is hard. Alone. Hungry. Occupied by bad television and relentless imaginings: an unforgiving, duty-filled future, changing my husband's diapers and hiding car keys. Sleep, despite pharmaceutical assistance, is often elusive.

"Do you think everything happens for a reason?" I ask Sister Jean, a sixty-ish nun, on a particularly rough night.

"Not really."

"You don't believe in fate? I thought that was a Catholic thing." She laughs.

"Oh good, I didn't offend you."

"Heavens, no. I'm not easily offended." She is hanging meds on the IV stand.

"Do you think God punishes us?"

"Do you feel like you're being punished?" Sister Jean perches on the chair next to my bed.

Excellent. I can use a therapy session right about now. "Maybe." I glance at the crucifix on the wall above my bed. (Lisa and I had laughed about it: "Do you think they'll be offended if we cover it up?" "I'll take all the help I can get.")

"Have you ever read *When Bad Things Happen to Good People* by Rabbi Harold Kushner?" she asks.

"Yes! You've read that?"

Sister Jean chuckles. "Our reading is non-denominational."

"I know. Sorry." I blush.

"No need to apologize. But as you may remember, the premise is that there's neither rhyme nor reason to why these things happen. But if the result is that these trials and tragedies motivate you to examine your path, to re-evaluate your direction and your choices, then at least some good can be derived from them."

Make good choices—a phrase I use repeatedly in parenting. Is this my purpose here? *Time to reflect, change my course? Take back my power, even in my frail, wasted state? Stop wallowing in self-pity? Re-commit to my husband, our family?*

"Break it off with Mark," Jesus—on the wall behind me—whispers. "Do it. Doesn't matter if you don't believe in me. Do the right thing."

"I'm not that strong yet," I whisper back.

Two of my closest friends, Jacie and Karen, want to visit. I am ashamed of how I look. I weigh a skeletal hundred pounds, feel like a pincushion, and haven't had a real shower or seen an ounce of makeup in the week I've been here.

After a few minutes of hospital small talk, they tell me I have an eating disorder. They've done some research and have found a day program at Stanford. I can come home at night to be with the kids. It's no worse than a full-time job, right? They will help with Hannah, Joshie, and David.

I'm cornered. *What the hell is this, an intervention? They're confronting me with this now?* Unable to escape, I listen patiently. I thank them profusely and gratefully for their love and courage.

I don't tell them that I stopped eating normally months earlier. That I was unhappy well before David's accident. That David's smoking (despite regularly promising to quit), constant sarcasm, and avoidance of household chores had driven a wedge between us. That I'm in love with another man.

The accident was just an additional excuse not to eat.

I tell them that I'll consider entering the program. I'll make getting healthy, getting strong, a priority. *So I can take care of everyone.*

They don't see me shaking my head as they leave. *Impossible. I'm not going into any stupid eating disorder program. Not going to happen.*

David's forty-fifth birthday is on June first, the day before I'm discharged. Lisa will take the kids and bring him his favorite spicy Chinese food after school. Hannah is making cupcakes. I feel negligent.

From my fifth floor room I can see Valley Med. I stand at my window, cell phone in hand, and pick out an arbitrary window. I imagine David sitting on his bed, perhaps dressed in jeans and his AMD T-shirt, frayed around the collar after hundreds of washings, hair growing back around the pronounced forehead scar.

The phone rings for a long time before he picks up.

"Hi, David, it's Rachel. Happy birthday."

"Rachel, my wife?"

"Yes, it's me. Sorry I can't come to see you today. I'm not sure if you know this, but I'm actually over at O'Connor. I've been in the hospital, too."

No response, other than the muffled sounds of daytime TV. *He doesn't care that you're sick. No, it's not that he doesn't care. Caring takes understanding, then processing, followed by feelings of compassion, sympathy. He doesn't have that capacity. Not anymore. He may never again have that capacity.*

"Do the nurses know it's your birthday? Are they doing anything special?"

Long silence. Then, "Let me think about it."

Eventually, I'll learn not to ask open-ended questions. Or if I do, to allow generous time and space for an answer. David can't process language or formulate a response in the back-and-forth style of ordinary conversation.

I plow ahead. I'm still learning.

"Lisa is bringing the kids to see you this afternoon. And when you come home—as soon as I'm out of here—we'll have that tiki party."

David was enamored with the culture, and for years had wanted a kitschy Polynesian-themed party—umbrella-topped rum-laced drinks, tiki torches, me in a grass skirt and coconut bra. We had named our cat Tiki for David's obsession, but never had the party. It was the least I could do for him now.

"Would you like that?"

"OK."

I've no idea what else to say. The urge to hang up is more powerful than my ability to keep this painful conversation—such as it is—going.

"OK, bye David. I hope to see you soon. And happy birthday."

I flip my phone shut and drag myself and my IV stand back to my bed.

This is my future. I better get used to it.

My husband has become a complete stranger.

·—·—·—·—·

HANNAHS SCHOOL JOURNAL ENTRY—
MAY 30, 2005
My family has very hard problems right now. It is because my dad is hurt, and my mom is in the hospital. But we are all happy my mom and dad are getting a lot better.

·—·—·—·—·

Lisa brings me home from the hospital after nine interminable days, a Thursday morning. The kids are in school, thank God. I have a few hours to catch my breath, reorient.

Priority:
- A shower.

Blessings:
- Using the toilet without needing a nurse to unhook my IV.
- Not being awakened at 6:00 a.m. by the painful jab of a blood draw needle.
- Wearing regular clothes.
- Eating regular food.
- Eating, period.

Undetermined:
- A restricted diet—especially no nuts, my favorite food, to prevent future diverticulitis attacks.
- Alcohol, at least not in front of David—he would want it and it could cause seizures.
- Financial conditions.
- Lawyers and lawsuits.

Determined:
- Being a full-time caregiver for two young children and a fully dependent unpredictable grown man.
- No privacy.
- No time to myself.
- Expected to have sex with a virtual stranger.

"Do you want me to stay for a while?" Lisa is putting away eggs, milk, apples in the refrigerator. "You going to be OK?"

"I think so." Much as I appreciate my sister, at that moment I just want her to leave, to process this transition alone.

And Mark is coming over.

As delicious hot water courses over my body, I study what's left. I'm lucky if my weight is in triple digits. Red track marks dot my arms and the backs of my hands and my neck from the central line needed when the veins in my arms or hands were no longer viable after days of needle sticks. I look like a junkie. In the tub, hunks of hair circle the drain like daddy long-legs.

Out of the shower, I wipe the foggy mirror. "Hellooo, gaw-geous," I say to my reflection in my best Barbra Streisand imitation.

Gorgeous? Not. I've never felt this ugly. Drained, empty, bony, frail. They took so much blood. Intestines weak and damaged, skin gray and flawed. Hair thin, straw-like, and lifeless. Huge eyes in a pinched, angular face.

Who is this woman?

. —.—.— —.

The next day, Lois saves my life.

It could be argued that I save my own life. I make the decision. But Lois opens the door, and I go through it. Her permission is my get-out-of-jail-free card.

I turn down Lois's offer of a soda from the vending machine. We're having a where-are-we-now-and-what's-next meeting on an outdoor terrace at Valley Med. The fog's lifted—it's a lovely California early summer morning.

She pulls two metal chairs under the shade of an umbrella, leans back to study me, shakes her head, and sighs. "My God, Rachel, you've had a rough time. How are you feeling now?"

Her genuine concern for me is surprising. Disconcerting. Until now we'd only discussed David's condition, David's needs. I don't answer right away, shifting uncomfortably as the bones of my ass dig into the unforgiving metal chair. Lois's eyes reflect the gaunt, skeletal creature in front of her. "Still pretty weak," I admit.

"The doctors say that for every day you spend in the hospital, it takes about ten days to fully recover." *Where she is going with this?* "You were there for nine days? Figure two to three months to get back to normal." I see her steal a glance at my bony arms, IV bruises, dull hair. "You need to take care of yourself."

I look at my left arm, clutch it protectively. *Take care of myself? How exactly? With my copious free time and excess millions of dollars? How the hell am I supposed to do that while caring for two kids and an impulsive, incontinent, seizure-prone grown man?* "Yeah." *That is so not going to happen. My sad little life is over. I'll even have to sneak drinks.*

Lois's focus is laser, blatant.

I shift again. *Damn, this chair is hard. Can she hear me whining about the lack of chardonnay in my future? Does she have any idea how selfish I really am? How cowardly? Can she guess that afternoons without my lover are more terrifying than my children losing a father or me a husband?*

"There is another option."

"I have options?" My creative imagination was stolen from the bag I put my clothes in at the ER.

"David doesn't have to come home."

I almost laugh out loud. *Seriously? No fucking way. I couldn't do that. What kind of a monster would refuse to care for her disabled husband? Not me, not a nice Jewish girl like me. I do the right thing. I fill the postman's bag with groceries. Buy unneeded gift-wrap from the neighbor's kid. Recycle. I will take care of my brain-injured husband, no matter how unhappy I've been in our marriage.*

"There's a facility in Gilroy called Learning Services. It's out in the country, kind of like a ranch. It's run by a lovely person— Dr. Jill Winegardner. She's Jewish, I think." Lois studies me. "She looks like you. I think you'd really like her."

It shouldn't have been reassuring that the director is Jewish. But it is. Lois is throwing me a lifeline—but all I can think about is Dr. Winegardner and I comparing matzah ball soup recipes.

Lois opens a folder, a brochure slides across the table.

She's been preparing for this conversation. She's been tracking my reality. I haven't been alone!

"They have a day program as well as live-in, but I'd recommend that David start with a few months in residence." So gentle. But so firm.

"But . . ."

She holds up her hand. "Just so you can regain your strength."

I allow myself to glance at the brochure, but quickly avert my eyes from that gateway to moral depravity. Yet, something shifts. In an instant I know I'm dangerously capable of considering her suggestion. Barely suspecting that my role as the heroine, the ingénue, the victim, is about to be usurped—just like Bette Davis in *All About Eve*.

This can work. No it can't. David can't go into an institution. Crazy people go into institutions, put there by selfish relatives who can't handle a little extra work. I can see the evil twin peeking from behind the curtain, stage left. The twin who would protest, "What about me? What about my life? My needs, my happiness? Don't I matter?"

Lois watches me wavering. She seizes her chance. "Your kids are so young. They are traumatized, too. They need a lot of support. The demands on you are going to be enormous. It would be insanely difficult in the best of circumstances—but you're weak, you're drained. You have no idea how often I've seen perfectly healthy caretakers implode from the stress." She moves in for the kill. "If you can't do it for yourself or David, do it for Hannah and Joshie."

My sore ass is forgotten. I lean forward. "Tell me more about Learning Services."

Chapter 9

IN THEATER, THE PERIOD BEFORE A show opens is "hell week." Usually the show is a hot mess as that week begins. Costumes don't fit, set pieces aren't finished, props are missing. One person can't remember lines. The stage manager is pissed off at the tech director because of a problem with the scrim, and the producer is haranguing everyone about slow ticket sales. Rehearsals run late into the night. Everyone is getting sick.

But opening night magic happens. Lines are remembered, set pieces function, pettiness is forgotten. Everyone pulls together for the cause. Somehow the show comes together.

My personal hell week runs in reverse—hopeful beginning, disastrous ending.

The phone rings at 7:15 a.m. while I'm pouring milk onto Joshie's cereal. "Don't want Cheerios," he whines. "I want cinnamon toast."

"Ask me in your normal voice and say please and I'll make some for you." I'm on autopilot—I've said that a thousand times before. "If you finish your Cheerios."

I grab the phone when it rings. Automatic. It's too early for sales calls.

"Rachel Michelberg?"

"Yes?" I'm wiping up milk from the counter.

"You're fucking my husband."

Oh my God. Diane.

The floor drops away, and I fall through space. I fight the impulse to empty the contents of my stomach—what little there is—and lean against the sink.

"I can't talk right now." My voice doesn't feel like it's coming out of me. "I'll call you back in a few hours." Like it was Sue or Lisa wanting to chat.

"You bitch. How do I know you'll call back?" Her voice is shrill. Venomous.

Hannah's brought her empty bowl to the sink and is looking at me curiously. "Mommy? You OK?" Joshie, as usual, is thankfully oblivious.

Hold it together. Don't let them know. They can't know.

I hold the phone away from my ear and put my hand over the mouthpiece. Diane is still shrieking. "Yes, honey, I'm fine. Get your backpack and help your brother find his."

Hannah scurries off to her room, and I slowly move the phone toward my ear.

"I promise I will call." She has every right to think I am full of shit. "I promise." I almost yell, as if saying it louder will be more convincing.

This will end badly, Mark had prophesied. In my blissful deluded state, I had no clue what badly might look like.

I manage to get the kids out the door and into the car. It's a miracle that I drive them safely to summer camp. Despite that miracle, my world as I knew it has just imploded. Again.

"Bye, guys. Remember your sunscreen!" I call as they scramble out of the car at the JCC drop-off area.

I have to talk to Mark. I pull into a parking space, punch in his number. My hands are trembling—I misdial twice.

"She knows everything," I tell him.

I should have foreseen his inane answer—"I know, and I'm sorry"—how weak and ineffectual he is. Not, "Are you OK?" or even, "I need to stay in my marriage." Nothing decisive, proactive. Not much said.

I make the decision—it's over. Absolutely, unequivocally over.

Relief. And panic. Having him in my life—and potentially more often in my bed—is the only thing that's just for me. Everything else drains me, demands attention and energy. Demands my very soul. David, the kids, my illness, finances, my job, the house. When Mark looks at me I feel beautiful. He reflects the sensuous, funny, talented, passionate, capable woman. Not the mother, laundress, cantor, wife, caregiver, housecleaner. He loves my voice—he understands it—musically and emotionally. David had stopped hearing it, hearing me—far back enough that I can't remember when I first noticed.

Fact: I cheated. Consequence: Diane's fury. I tell my kids that if you cheat, you'll get caught and be punished. There are consequences. Cheating is bad. Cheating is wrong.

I'm paralyzed, staring at the phone in my hand. Once I dial, it's really over. No more guilt, at least not about this relationship. Ending it is a good thing, the right thing. It will heal me. *Do it.*

I consider driving home to be in a safe, protected place before calling, but I might lose my nerve. I gaze out the side window at a line of four-year-olds holding hands in pairs as they walk toward the pool, each with a towel. So sweet, their innocence, their purity. I squint. The window's grimy. How long has it been since I stopped at a carwash?

Get it over with. I press redial, hand shaking as I bring the phone to my ear. I press harder, as if the phone will drop from sheer terror.

"Diane, this is Rachel Michelberg." Why am I saying my full name? Perhaps I'm already reclaiming my identity?

She tries to talk, but I don't let her—I'm in a hurry. I want it to end—all of it. The sneaking around, the lies, the guilt, this call. Especially this call.

"It's over. I'll never see him again. I promise. You have no reason to believe me but it's really true. I can't handle any of this."

I stop myself from launching into my sob story—as if she'd have compassion for my situation. My actions. Do I really think she'll hear my pain? Understand—even a little—why I strayed, why I fell in love with her husband?

Whatever she snarls in response, amounts to I'm a bitch and full of shit.

I'm coherent, I say what I need to say. I hang up on her. There's no point in prolonging a sordid drama unless there's a brilliant composer enlivening the libretto. Mostly there's silence. Outside and in. In a definitive way I feel truly unburdened.

For about two minutes. Until the loneliness descends like a giant hand squeezing my throat. No more rushing home to read gooey emails. No more bottomless brown eyes gazing into mine. No more deep conversations about Stravinsky and Schumann.

No one putting me at the center of his universe.

Back home, I sit on the sofa. The house is quiet. Tiki nuzzles my hand. I scratch his head, he purrs. My eyes are oddly dry. Perhaps there's nothing left.

"So, Tiki, how's your day going?" His tail flicks. "Thanks for asking, dude. Me, I'm talking to a cat. That pretty much sums it up."

Alcoholics and addicts refer to "hitting bottom." The classic scenario: You wake up lying in a dark alley, sticky with your own vomit. It's raining. There's no one left to call for help. You're alone, empty, broke, and humiliated. You've lost everything to your addiction. There's nowhere to go but up.

Or down.

Even though I'm sitting in my clean dry living room, in my clean dry clothes, petting my clean purring cat, I realize I'm hitting bottom—for the second time in ten days. "Let go and let God" they say in 12-step. I have to let Mark go. I have to stop trying to control everything. I have to let go of my life as I've known it.

There will be no flowers, no accolades, for this opening night.

. ——. — —.

HANNAH'S SCHOOL JOURNAL ENTRY—
JUNE 9, 2005

I am sad. My dad is not going to come home. He was supposed to come home last Saturday. But even worse is that he won't come home for a couple weeks. He will be in a place like a farm in Gilroy. That means I won't be able to see him that much. I hope he comes back before my birthday. I love my father!

. ——. — —.

Lois arranges for me to visit Learning Services. It's not exactly in the middle of nowhere, but it's close. Officially, it's in Gilroy, an agricultural town about a half hour south of San Jose, but the downtown area (mainly strip malls and chain stores) is not within walking distance. Set back from the road, with no sign marking its location, Learning Services is comprised of a few drab one-story buildings—a sort of wannabe farm with nothing growing (aside from a meager vegetable garden) and no animals other than a couple of house cats.

I instantly like Dr. Winegardner, the director. *Winegardner. Meant to be? David did crash into a vineyard.* Kind, compassionate, seems to know her stuff. She gives me a tour, greeting the residents. It's comforting to see that she knows all their names. I try to imagine David there. He's a city guy—enjoys dressing up, going to clubs, good restaurants. He also loves getting down and dirty in nature—but this place is neither city nor truly country.

It's only temporary. It will have to work. There are no other facilities close enough to visit regularly. We schedule David's admission for the following Tuesday.

On Monday, he has a massive seizure.

Not surprising, the doctors tell me. It probably won't be the last one. David needs to remain in the hospital until he's medically stable.

As if I don't have enough guilt, I'm ecstatic for the reprieve from making a decision. David stays at Valley Med. I'm off the hook. *Thank you, David. Maybe in a weird way you're watching out for me?*

. — .—. — . —.

The kids and I resume our routine prior to my hospitalization. Taxi them to summer camp, consult with doctors, David's therapies. Working at the temple, tutoring Bar and Bat Mitzvah students when I can. Swimming and piano lessons, karate, gymnastics. Back to Valley Med for the kids to visit David. At night we watch *Project Runway* or *Whose Line Is It Anyway?* Fluffy, funny TV is our medicine, our panacea.

I think that—as it has for most of my life—doing a show will bring me joy. I audition for my favorite role, Carmen. I don't get the part. Later, the director explains that I looked so frail she was afraid to cast me.

I try to eat but can hardly choke down even Ensure protein drinks.

I try not to cry constantly. I miss Mark so much.
I realize I also miss David.

. — .— . — —.

During my daily visits I often notice a man in the ward who's visiting his brain-injured girlfriend. I see them together in the visiting room, on the terrace, in physical therapy, the cafeteria. Neither of them is wearing a ring. Mid-thirties. It's clear she'd been beautiful, but now she looks strange, contorted, fragile in her wheelchair. I wonder about their story. How long had they been dating? Was he about to propose? How did her brain injury happen—riding on the back of his motorcycle? Is that why he's so attentive?

I'm horrified to find myself attracted to him. I'm dying to connect, to bond over the crisis we share, our mutual misery. *If I just introduce myself . . . no, that's going too far. Maybe just flirt a little—God, that's reprehensible. Besides, he only has eyes for her. Look at how he looks at her, how caring he is. But will he stick it out? Will he stay with her? Of course he will, he is a saint, a mensch. I'm evil. Maybe not evil, but definitely not a mensch. And very far from sainthood.*

I'm jealous of her. *How screwed up is that?*

. — .— . — —.

HANNAH'S SCHOOL JOURNAL ENTRY—JUNE 1
I can't wait because on June 3rd and 4th I will be in a gymnastics show. It is Hawaiian. It will be so fun because people will be watching me and I will be dancing. But I am glad Esther will be in it with me in the big show. Being in a show is the best! But even better is that I get to wear a special leotard. I can't wait!

. _. _. _ . _ .

At Hannah's gymnastics show I comprehend the extent of our loss at an infinitely deeper level.

Lisa and Gordon meet Joshie and me at the gym. They've been there actively for us—visiting David, driving kids, running errands. Gordon makes a point of playing with Joshie—ping-pong, trips to the ice-cream store, swimming. Their son Aaron, on the competitive gymnastics team, is also performing, but they come to this show mostly for Hannah. For me.

From the bleachers, I gaze down on the leotard-clad six- and seven-year-olds performing their newfound skills. All around cameras flash, camcorders whirr—hundreds of proud dads. I'm not prepared for the wallop of sadness. I pull Joshie onto my lap and bury my wet face in his golden curls. He and his sister will never have that again. There will never be anyone except me to *kvell*—to burst with pride at their smallest accomplishment, their most rudimentary somersault or balancing on a beam six inches from the floor.

I see Gordon and Lisa smiling and applauding when Hannah executes a perfectly awkward cartwheel. They will be there for her, for Joshie.

But it's not the same.

It's all up to me now—the cheering, the scolding, the *kvelling*, the loving, the teaching, along with cleaning up the messes, taking out the garbage. The hopes and dreams that only parents can have for their children. The disappointments—mine alone.

I'm a single parent. I knew it before, but now it is real—achingly real.

Joshie squirms from my grasp and asks for water. I watch him drink from the plastic bottle, thinking, *I can't do this.*

. —.—. — — .

David needs another surgery. The cause of his seizure has been determined as pneumocephalus, a CSF leak—cerebral-spinal fluid collecting in the brain causing pressure on the brain stem. The neurosurgeon will insert a permanent shunt extending from his brain into his belly, where the fluid will be absorbed.

But the six-hour surgery won't improve brain function, just reduce the likelihood of seizures. *Would David have wanted it?* I wouldn't if it were me.

The procedure is successful, but a few weeks later David develops a highly contagious hospital-induced viral infection. Isn't he dealing with enough already?

Aren't I?

The treatment: a special antibiotic that the infection is not yet resistant to—plus isolation. Anyone entering the room must wear a gown and mask, use hand sanitizer. The children's visits must be severely restricted.

I plan to spend some time with David that July morning, then try to get some work done at the temple before collecting the kids.

I greet the nurses. David has been moved around so much—from the ICU when he first arrived at Valley Med, to the TBI rehab unit, the medical unit after his seizure, post-op, and now back to the ICU. I've stopped trying to remember the nurses' names.

"How's he doing? Any changes since last night?"

"Disoriented, but otherwise stable. He keeps trying to leave."

"How long do you think before he can be transferred out of here?" I'm clumsily donning the papery yellow gown that ties in the back. Maybe it's laziness or feeling awkward with arms raised over my head to tie it, but I usually leave it untied, creating a slouchy, tenty look.

"Hard to say." The nurse looks thoughtful. I'm used to vague responses. Maybe they're afraid I'll sue them if they give me a definite answer that doesn't materialize. "Another four or five days at least. A full twenty-four hours after his tests are all clear."

"Thanks." I smile at her, adjusting the gown/tent over my clothes. I strap on the face mask and approach the door to David's room. I sigh—yes, I knew about the twenty-four hour rule. How many times have I heard it? They mean well, but it feels patronizing. The seed of cynicism and intolerance that can linger for months, years, has already sprouted a thriving plant.

I reach for the door handle, pause. *Breathe.* The visits are hard. No, torturous. David is again a pincushion of IVs. Machines blink and beep endlessly. The harsh fluorescent light is a constant reminder that none of this is natural—the room, the hospital, this ridiculous, awful situation.

It isn't supposed to be this way—even if we were unhappy. Maybe I sometimes wanted out of my marriage. Maybe, when David had stepped over the kids' toys without thinking to pick them up once too often (after sleeping in as I got the kids ready while preparing for work), I even fantasized about divorce—I could be free. That thought usually lasted for about ten seconds. *Stop it. Stop it! He's a good guy. He's a great father. Everyone has problems, every married couple on the planet. This is normal!*

This isn't anywhere close to normal.

"Hi, David!" I say brightly. "How's it going?"

What a stupid, stupid question. But what else do you say?

The bed is propped up in a slightly reclining position. David's head is slack to one side, eyes closed. His hair has started growing back after the surgery and is framing the brand-new scar almost purposely, as if to announce: Look at this great scar! Look what I survived! Look how messed up my life will be now!

"David," I stand at the foot of the bed after dumping my purse on the window ledge and shake his foot gently. "C'mon, wake up. I brought some nail clippers."

David blinks and pulls his foot away. He peers at me, both eyes squinting. Even the sightless right eye. "Are you Hannah? Where's Rachel?"

"I'm Rachel. Your wife. Hannah's at camp." I head back to my purse to retrieve the tools I've brought for the pedicure—thick foot cream in addition to the clippers. Despite lack of use—or perhaps because of it—David's feet are worn, cracked, dry. The nails are so long they're starting to curl around his toes. David wasn't overly fastidious, but he cared deeply about hygiene and fashion. He favored Italian shoes and German suits. He scheduled haircuts every three weeks (more often than I thought necessary), and he always insisted the back of his neck be shaved clean. I did it for him between haircuts.

I'm remembering how fresh and soft his neck looked after I'd wiped off the remnants of shaving cream. How handsome he was.

And I'm remembering how I'd tease him when his too-long toenails scratched my shins as we made love. "Ow!" I'd whine. "You've GOT to cut your nails!"

"I took care of my toes," he'd say the next day, hopefully.

I sit on the edge of the bed and start removing his socks, grateful for the diversion. Usually the visits are labored, painfully silent aside from the drone of daytime TV. This is something I can do. It's one way—one pathetic way—I can do something to take care of him.

Carefully I start cutting. He's passive at first, but soon becomes resistant, either jerking his foot away or tensing it so much I can't get to the toes. "David, it's OK. I'm almost done." It isn't true, but I don't know how else to soothe him.

"You can't do that," an edge to his voice I haven't heard since the crash. "You're not supposed to do that."

Suddenly the clippers dive into the fleshy part of David's toe. He yelps, kicking my hand and knocking the clippers to the floor.

"Oh shit, I'm sorry. So sorry!" I'm babbling. "It was an accident. Let me find something to stop the bleeding." I scoop up the clippers and head to the sink for a towel. *What an idiot. I can't even cut his goddamn nails without screwing up.*

My mind has hoarded a memory of being at a resort in Mexico and trying to trim toddler Joshie's fingernails. He's flailing his fists and screaming in protest, just like he does at the barber's. I croon, cajole, offer lollipops. He won't be soothed. "Please, Joshie. I'm almost done." Blood gushes from his middle finger—the cut so deep he'll need stitches. Screaming turns into agonizing howls. I've inflicted pain on my baby. I'm an unfit mother.

Gently I press the washcloth around David's toe. "It's not too bad. I'm really sorry. I should have been more careful." Babbling again.

David studies me. "You always were a bitch."

There is no emotion in his tone. Matter-of-fact. His truth of the moment. Or has this always been how he felt? Is the TBI like a truth serum? The filtering frontal lobe has been shredded apart like grated cheese. What if it has uncovered reality instead of altering it?

We'd had an awful fight two days before the accident. I'd just returned from singing in a concert in LA. David asked me to stay with him for a few days the following week at the Hayes Mansion, a beautiful hotel and conference center in San Jose where he was organizing a work conference.

It had been a superhuman effort to organize childcare just for a few days in LA. "Are you kidding me?" I'd hissed. "Do you know how hard it is for me to get away? Why don't *you* make all of the childcare arrangements?!"

David had backed off, crestfallen.

He'd tried to do something nice, something loving. Why the pugnacious reaction? I was completely unreasonable that night. I *was* a bitch at times.

"I'm sorry, David." I bandage his toe. "I'm so sorry—for everything."

His blank look tells me it's obvious that he has no idea what I'm talking about. I'm not about to remind him of that fight, nor the bloody toe.

In the end, neither of us made it to the Hayes Mansion.

Chapter 10

I'M BECOMING A SURVIVAL MODE EXPERT. My strategies:

- Yoga. Cry all over the mat during random asanas. Child's pose especially weep-worthy.
- Therapy. Cry some more.
- Invite friends over. Drink chardonnay. Cry.

Money is a constant worry. David's company Passavé had kept him on salary for a few months, but that period is coming to a close. Shortly before the accident, David and I agreed that I could quit the synagogue to invest energy in theater and opera—my first love. I would establish a private voice teaching studio to cover the shortfall. I'd given notice at the temple, effective after the High Holy Days in September.

I'm told to apply for Social Security for the kids, and manage to jump through enough hoops and red tape to dress the whole cast of *The Marriage of Figaro*. It's not nearly enough.

I allow myself to hope for a positive financial resolution of the personal injury lawsuit, despite no guarantees and no idea of the timing. The hundreds of thousands of dollars in bills for ambulances, surgeons, assessments, and hospitals are mounting. I learn I shouldn't have given our personal health insurance information to the hospital in San Luis Obispo; I should have filed a workers' comp claim. That mistake is fixable, but a colossal pain to correct. Lois hadn't yet entered my life, and I'd been all reactivity.

Suze Orman's proselytizing for independence and being prepared—particularly for women—had never penetrated my marriage. I'd turned over our financials, legal issues, credit card tracking, passwords, insurance policies, and Quicken systems to David, rationalizing my abdication of that responsibility to the true fact that he was better at it anyway and I had no head for numbers.

Now I'm facing a customer service rep.

Me: "Hi, I need to get some information regarding the coverage on my policy."

Customer Service Rep: "Do you have the PIN number on that account?"

Me (sighing): "No, I'm sorry. That's why I'm calling. I can't log in to do it online because I don't have the password or the PIN. You may not believe this but my husband was in an airplane crash and . . ."

CSR: "Oh I'm so sorry. Is he deceased?"

Me: "No, but he's not capable of managing our affairs, and I need access to our account."

CSR: "Hmmm."

Me: "I know it doesn't sound like the truth, I'm really not making this up . . ."

CSR: "Your birthdate please?"

Several methods of identification later—and supervisors consulted—access is granted.

What marital fantasy had distracted us from a little just-in-case planning?

. —.—. — —.

The shunt surgery has brought David's seizures under control, but he's still too unstable to move to Learning Services—his condition requires a lower patient-staff ratio than they can provide. Lois recommends Neurobehavioral Cognitive Services (NCS). It's a small residential facility in Dixon, a rural farming community in California's central valley, a ninety-minute drive from home, but not far from where Mom lives in Benicia. She and I can go during the week and bring the kids on weekends.

Lois thinks it's a good solution. I concur. Arrangements are made. David will be transferred within the month.

. —.—. — —.

Everyone grills me about how the kids are doing, always the first question they ask after inquiring about David. So innocent, so caring, so gentle. So predictable. Yet I never know how to answer. Shitty? Fine? Managing? Resilient? All of the above? In truth I have no capacity to deal with Hannah and Joshie's emotional health, beyond loving them, meeting daily needs, and keeping their lives as normal as possible. I'm told I'll "just know" when it's time to get them some therapy.

Late July. It's hot as hell in our cute but pre-war house. The few ceiling fans pant to stir the smallest breeze. I let the kids off kitchen duty. I want to be alone, have a reprieve from their bickering. They're watching *High School Musical* for the hundredth time. "Get your head in the game," sings Zac Efron, his teenage angst particularly irritating as I rinse forks and dishes. The pockmarks on the vinyl floor and dingy tile grout add to my annoyance at the goddamned useless fan.

Suddenly I'm gulping, sobbing, choking. I hate this kitchen. Hate the dirty forks. Hate Zac Efron. Hate David for doing this to me. Hate Mark for keeping a hold on my heart. Most of all hate myself for being so powerless.

"Mommy? What's wrong? Why are you crying?" Hannah can feel my meltdown from the next room. She comes in and hugs me.

Caught. I try so hard not to let them see me cry. "I'm OK, honey." *Stupid lie.* "I'm sad about Daddy." I manage to be truthful. Could filthy grout make tears erupt?

Hannah is pure compassion. She leans back, her little arms sweet around my waist, and looks up at me. "You don't have to cry on the outside. You can cry on the inside. That's what I do when I'm sad about Daddy." *Jesus. How long has she felt this way?*

The next day I book her a therapy appointment.

－－－－－－－

A letter arrives, announcing that David's driver's license must be surrendered to the DMV by a certain date. Not "handed over." Surrendered. As if David has committed a crime.

I don't procrastinate—he's never going to sit behind the wheel of car again. Not if he's incapable of controlling impulses nor remembering to use the toilet.

At the DMV, I'm directed to a window with a short line. I glance at the bored, frustrated people waiting in other lines: the young mother trying to entertain a squirmy toddler, the suited business guy on his phone, the nervous teenager about to take her driving test.

"Next customer," the clerk drones.

"Hi, I'm supposed to turn in my husband's license."

He extends his hand without looking up. "Do you have a letter?"

I give it to him.

"License please." His eyes stay on the computer screen.

I dig in my purse for my wallet. Placing the license on the counter, I see David's blue, pre-accident, fully-seeing eyes smiling up at me. His smooth, crevasse-free forehead.

Tears well. The clerk reaches for the license. I don't let it go. "This is really hard. It's my husband. His name is David. He was in a plane crash. He has a brain injury. He'll never drive again." I struggle to hold in the deluge. Uselessly. I'm having yet another meltdown.

The clerk looks like he would prefer to be anywhere else.

I fish for a tissue in my purse. "I'm sorry. I didn't know this would be so hard. David can't do anything by himself. He's only forty-five. He can't even be left alone."

The clerk glances around.

"He's not an adult anymore."

"Do you need to sit down?"

God, I'm making a scene. "No thanks. I'm OK. Sorry. TMI, I guess." A little snort escapes, a laugh/cry. *Pull yourself together.* "Do you need anything else?" I'm feeling a little sorry for the clerk, alone with this crazy lady.

He pushes a piece of paper toward me. "Sign this release form, please."

I sign and blow my nose.

"Next in line."

Dismissed. I start to leave. I turn back. The clerk is already helping the next person. I look at the young mother, her toddler examining his bag of Goldfish crackers.

"He used to be a really good driver," I say to no one in particular.

._____

August sixth, my birthday and the sixtieth anniversary of the bombing of Hiroshima. NPR is playing reminiscences throughout the day. Stories of horrible disfigurations, lives lost, whole families obliterated.

I should feel lucky. My problems are so small in comparison.

I want to feel lucky, even happy. My children are intact. My intestines are healing—I'm even gaining some weight. David is alive, progressing enough to leave the hospital. I'm not feeling the tiniest bit grateful. Just empty and tired. And terrified.

The gifted spa treatment and dinner out with friends that night are a Band-Aid on a gaping wound.

David is moved to NCS later that week. The kids and I pick up Mom and visit on the weekend. NCS is homey, warm even, with cushy outdated plaid sofas and throw rugs. The large farmhouse has been converted into a private residential TBI facility. We play Chutes and Ladders, Sorry, and Candyland and stay for dinner—bland chicken, salad, garlic bread. David is more relaxed, less agitated, relatively passive. The caretakers tell me that he allows them to guide him for ADLs—Activities of Daily Living: dressing, showering, toileting. While the kids play games with David, one of the occupational therapists shows Mom and me the laminated card he uses in the shower.

1. Turn on the water
2. Undress
3. Test the water for temperature

4. Step into the shower
5. Wet hair and body
6. Lather body with soap, rinse
7. Shampoo, rinse
8. Apply conditioner, rinse
9. Turn off water
10. Step out of shower
11. Dry body and hair

"We cue him the whole time. Showering doesn't seem like a very complicated activity, but it really is. The brain has to manage following several steps in the right order. If we don't remind him to use the card and cue him to follow the steps, he'll perseverate—for example, shampooing five times but not washing his body at all, or forgetting to rinse."

Perseveration, confabulation, ADLs. A whole vocabulary I never wanted to learn. I am grateful for these professionals and their expertise. Despite my despair, I marvel at the wonders of the brain. How we take it for granted. How complex functioning independently is.

Mom gazes at me with that combination of pity, sadness, and false optimism I've come to expect. She wants to be the rock I need.

There's very little she, or anyone, can do.

* * *

A new disaster, one with a name: Katrina. We watch those unfortunate souls in faraway New Orleans waiting to be rescued from rooftops or crammed into the Astrodome—hungry, anxious, thirsty, hot. Hannah is upset; Joshie barely registers the scope of the tragedy.

I take the opportunity, with Hiroshima fresh in mind, as a teaching moment. "Those poor people have lost their homes, maybe even members of their family. We're so lucky. We have our house, and each other."

"Stop it, Joshie!" Hannah screeches as he hurls himself off the arm of the living room sofa onto its cushions. Joshie scrambles back to his launch pad. Hannah strokes Tiki's fur. "And animals? Did the animals get killed, too?"

"Yes, honey. Some of the animals died. But I'm sure many were also saved." I want her to connect with the fifteen pounds of soft, living cat. To sense the comfort he offers. To appreciate the relationships in her life, while she has them.

Every Monday Hannah and I go to her therapy appointment. Though I'm dying to listen in on the sessions, instead I wander the posh, overpriced Los Gatos shops usually resisting the urge to buy anything more than a cup of coffee.

"It was OK. We played some games," says Hannah, shoveling Cold Stone cookie dough ice cream into her mouth. "Am I seeing Sonya next Monday, too? I like getting out of school early."

Not much information there. Sonya's told me that the main goal is to create a safe environment for Hannah to express herself. I have to abdicate control. At the least, we spend time together without sibling squabbles, without Joshie constantly demanding my attention.

──────

Joshie is entering first grade, and I still haven't decided on a school.

A few months before his fourth birthday, the preschool director voiced some concerns at a parent-teacher conference. Joshie is a bright, sweet child, she said. Inquisitive, sensitive, talented, with excellent small motor skills. But she noticed some odd social behaviors—following children around the playground repeating, "What's your name?" until they ran away in frustration. Fixating on certain activities, organizing and rearranging blocks and foam letters obsessively. His language development wasn't at age level. He's easily overstimulated and has regular meltdowns.

David and I consulted a psychiatrist who concluded that Joshie is on the autism spectrum. Asperger's syndrome. On a scale of one to ten, he was a seven or eight.

Joshie isn't re-tested. He does better at the temple preschool. His language progresses. He has a few friends. Now facing first grade, I should start the testing process, but the mere thought of the scheduling, paperwork, and finding an appropriate school makes me hyperventilate. Not to mention the probable confirmation of the autism diagnosis.

Whether I choose the smart way or the easy way, I decide that Joshie will attend first grade at Yavneh, the Jewish Day School where Hannah will be in third grade. She loved the first grade teacher and the class size is small. I worry that Yavneh, like most private schools, can't accommodate special needs children well, but my bandwidth to research other options is nonexistent. I take the leap of faith that Joshie will be alright.

. — . — . — . — . .

I receive a call from Noam, an acquaintance from the temple. His daughter will be chanting Torah for the Yom Kippur service, and he wants to schedule a tutoring session.

"Oh my God. I heard what happened." Noam's accent is thick with concern. "How are you holding up?"

He's a large, jovial man with a shaved head and flirtatious ways that are strangely acceptable from an Israeli who was a tank driver in the army. He has the demeanor and disposition of a puppy. I find him oddly attractive.

"Surviving. I've been better."

We schedule his daughter's appointment and chat for a few minutes—about his job and kids, the temple, the finalization of his acrimonious divorce.

"If there's anything I can do for you, please don't hesitate to call."

"Well, actually—there is. You can take me out to dinner."

What did I just say? Yet I immediately sense the kind of contentment that comes only from speaking truth.

"Well, um—sure. Of course."

"If you don't feel comfortable . . . I mean, I'm still married to David, but he's not really . . ."

Not really what? What would I have said if he hadn't interrupted my explanation?

"No, no, I understand. I'd love to take you to dinner. In fact, I'm honored."

I toy with my wedding ring as we set a time after Yom Kippur.

I'll take it off when Noam and I go out. But I'll put it on again right afterward. It's not as if I'm hiding anything from him.

I have a date.

⸻

I sing my last High Holidays at the temple, emotionally removed from the intended piety in the sanctuary. It's hard work managing the choir and accompanist, staying alert for cues—and vocally demanding. These tasks justify my lack of spiritual attachment. This year, I'm even more distant. David has been on the *R'fuah Sh'leyma* roster—congregants who are ill and "in need of spiritual healing." Every Friday night I listen to his name read aloud, eyes glued to my *siddur*, my prayer book, to avoid sympathetic glances. I appreciate the sentiment and acknowledge that prayers can't hurt, but I've never believed they cure.

This year, I not only feel detached. I'm a fraud, a poster child for sin. What right do I, the adulteress—in my symbol of purity lily-white polyester robe—have to speak to God on behalf of the congregation? Hester Prynne is a more fitting role.

For the sins we have committed against you, we ask Adonai for forgiveness:

Ashamnu—*We have trespassed.*
He'evinu—*We have acted perversely.*
V'hirshanu—*We have done wrong.*
Tafalnu sheker—*We have spoken falsehood.*
Rashanu—*We have acted wickedly.*
Tainu—*We have gone astray.*

Ay yay yay, the song keens in mournful melody. The congregation echoes each sin, symbolically rapping the knuckles of our right hand against our hearts.

We have a different musician this year (thank God I had the foresight to hire someone else) but I feel Mark's presence on the *bimah*, missing him with an intensity that surprises me, even in this moment desire outweighs guilt. After the confessional, I silently swear. *Get the fuck out of my head. You're not welcome here. In this sanctuary, in my thoughts.*

- - - - - - -

David is settling into his existence at NCS, passively. Not much cognitive improvement, but he complies with the therapy protocols. The incontinence is getting worse. He's cued every hour to use the bathroom, but it doesn't always work. I take the kids to visit David every other weekend, Mom and I cover alternate weeks. As we head to the car after the visit, I'm relieved to leave. Every single time.

My brother Paul and his wife Susie take their kids, eight-month-old Sierra and seven-year-old Jackson, to visit David. David wants to hold Sierra. "Give her to me, give her to me." Susie is reluctant but puts Sierra on David's lap. He bounces her on his knee, singing "Hannah, Hannah, Hannah-ley . . . you are so pretty."

"This isn't Hannah, David. It's Sierra, our baby." Paul glances at Susie.

David becomes agitated. They have to cut their visit short.

. — . — . — — . .

My therapist Nancy, who's known me since I was a teenager, cuts into my unusual silence. "What are you feeling right now?"

"Shame."

If she's surprised, she doesn't show it. "What are you ashamed of?"

I hesitate, biting the inside of my lips—hard. I've been telling Nancy my darkest secrets for almost thirty years. What am I afraid of? That she'll fire me as a client?

"I'm relieved when David isn't improving. Because if he gets better I'll have to take him home."

Only five minutes into our session and I break into deep, wailing howls. She pushes the tissue box across the table.

"I don't want to take care of him. I don't think I can do it." Choking sobs, inhaling snot and tears. "As long as he's incapacitated, so . . . sick, with the incontinence and seizures, you know, those really serious issues, I feel like I'm justified. But if he gets better . . ."

"If he gets better?" Nancy prompts, when my voice trails off.

"Dora and Sigi will expect me to take him home."

Nancy leans back, eyebrows raised, the expression I know well when I've gotten to the truth. "Yes, they will. But it's your life, Rachel. You know you can't live it to please your in-laws."

"I know. But David . . ."

"David will be cared for. You're doing everything you can—everything within your capacity—to make sure of that. You're recognizing your own limitations. That's a show of strength."

"Exactly. My limitations. I should be able to take care of him. Dora would do it if it were her husband."

"I shouldn't have used that word. Let me put it another way—you're acknowledging your boundaries. You might not have accepted them yet, but it's the first step. You know you'll implode if David is home. That you could easily fall back into your eating disorder. Or become an alcoholic. Like your mother."

Implode. The same word Lois used. Collapse, shrink, cave in. My own crash.

". . . or get into an unhealthy relationship with a married man," I say. *As if there's a healthy version.*

I study the bookcase on the wall behind Nancy. Hundreds of books. My eyes wander over *Zen and the Art of Motorcycle Maintenance*, *Passages*, *The Drifters*. As usual, I wonder how many of them she's actually read.

I add another crumpled, wet Kleenex to the growing pile on the coffee table. "I keep wondering if things would be different if our marriage had been strong. If I'd been happy with David."

"I know. But it wasn't. You have to live your truth, your reality. Give yourself permission to not be a superhero."

Lois again. *Are these two in cahoots?*

"What I'm hearing," she continued, "is that you're not in love with David anymore, but you still care about him deeply, and you want him to get the best treatment possible. You can't be his caretaker *and* take care of yourself. Perhaps Dora could. But you're not Dora." Nancy uncrosses her legs and leans forward. For a moment I think she's going to take my hand. "Remember the diverticulitis attack. If something happens to you, emotionally or physically, who will take care of Hannah and Joshie?"

She has said the magic words.

She's right.

I'm moving ever closer to the decision that will drive David's family to combat.

. —.—. — —.

JOSHIE'S SCHOOL JOURNAL

I practice to be a black belt in Karate. I go two times a week. When I am older I get a lot of new belts until black. I have to pay attention to my instructor. Next belt I am getting is yellow, which I am winning next Thursday. Right now I am on a white belt. I earn lots of checks and stripes. I love Karate.

. —.—. — —.

Six months already and the lawsuit is only in the discovery phase—researching the cause of the accident, what actually caused the engine to malfunction, who might be liable, hoping that the responsible party has "deep pockets." I hate that last idea—associate it with sleaziness, avarice, corruption. Now I'm the one with my hand out, looking for a well to dig.

I meet my lawyer Mike for lunch to discuss. He's learned that the plane had last been serviced at Aviation Classics, a tiny maintenance facility in Reno, Nevada. "A popsicle stand. If it's their fault, we're screwed."

I'm confused. *Someone has to pay for this.*

Mike takes a sip of his Arnold Palmer. "Aviation Classics doesn't have any assets. They could sell everything off and it wouldn't even be a drop in the bucket. At least David's medical bills will be covered by workers' comp."

Thank God. Otherwise, I'd be forced to sell our house—which still wouldn't cover David's future expenses. I need to make money. We have some savings, the kids' dependent Social Security is now coming in, some freelance calls are coming from other temples. It isn't enough. Will my old synagogue take me back? The nights and weekends required would be brutal. I'd have to procure childcare. And they've already hired someone else.

I'll figure something out. We have to stay in the house. The kids need consistency. And I love our neighborhood, the old sycamore trees, our neighbors Joe and Mary, walking to the park and the bank.

I look up. "Workers' comp will cover him for the rest of his life, right?"

"Yup." Mike smiles with palpable confidence. "But we're going to try and get David—and you and the kids—more." His firm is on a generous contingency, a strong incentive. "You need to be patient," he advises. "These cases can take a long time."

"Months?"

This time his smile is apologetic. "Years."

I think of Dory in *Finding Nemo. Just keep swimming.* But these waters are ever murkier.

－－－－－－－

I'm giddy preparing for my date, hiding my anticipation from the kids. Mom will babysit, knowing my secret, happy to see me happy if just for a little while.

I've instructed Noam not to come to the door. He takes me to a French restaurant. I'm relaxed, flirtatious, enjoying the male company. Noam plays right along. My excitement surprises me. It's not about the potential sex. When Noam gazes at me, his gold-green eyes appreciating what he sees, I realize how desperately I've missed being looked at that way. My body has been an albatross—skinny but not beautiful. Hungry but little pleasure in eating.

A few days later, when the kids are at school, we meet at his house on his lunch break and we make love. It feels so good I'm in tears afterward. At least I think that's why I weep.

Chapter 11

DORA CALLS REGULARLY FOR UPDATES. She's planning to come for a few weeks in December. In the meantime, her 21-year-old middle daughter who's just completed her army service is coming to help me out.

Tammy is delightful—funny, upbeat, a hard worker. The kids adore their cousin, but I'm unsure how much to confide in her. We have some honest conversations about my predicament—I even confess that I'm not sure if I will bring David home. "Please don't tell your mom. I haven't made a final decision yet. Besides, I want to tell her myself."

Tammy nods in agreement. I suspect Dora won't be as understanding.

With the kids off school for Sukkot, the Jewish harvest festival, we all pile in the car and drive to Disneyland. They're too short for Space Mountain or the Matterhorn, but Tammy takes them on the Teacups and Splash Mountain while I happily wave from the safety of the sidelines. I haven't seen their smiles so wide, their joy so unbridled, for months.

Back home, Noam comes for dinner. I introduce him to the kids as "a friend from the temple." He and Tammy instantly bond, chattering away in Hebrew while I cook. It almost feels like a normal family.

Tammy encourages me to go out with him. "I'll take care of the kids, no problem. We don't have to tell them what you're doing."

I love Tammy. It's like having a gal-pal, maid, and nanny wrapped into one non-judgmental package. Noam is crazy about her. We're both depressed when she goes back to Israel. It's as if we sense that Tammy leaving—and Dora arriving—will lead to the end of our relationship, which in fact is exactly what happens. It is just too hard for me to get away.

. —. —. . — . . —.

"Is there a room where Rachel and I can have some privacy?" Lois asks the NCS staffer. She and his case manager are observing David as I show him some of the kids' school artwork and a story Hannah has written. He can read—but not follow the plot. The conversation afterward is limited and stilted. Most of the time we just sit while I fumble for a way to relate to him.

"What did you do yesterday?" I ask, forgetting that open-ended questions lead to nowhere.

David pauses, his dented brow furrowing. I can almost see the synapses in his brain firing, trying desperately to connect the mangled, obstructed pathways.

After a few moments his good eye lights up. "Stuart and I went clubbing. Then we had pho at the Cambodian place!"

I sigh. He has never gone clubbing with Stuart. Stuart doesn't go to nightclubs. But they did meet often at a Cambodian restaurant for lunch. A sign of progress?

He appears happy with those memories, as faulty as they are. Yesterday—a routine day—he probably did physical therapy, perhaps played a cognitive computer game, took a cue-driven shower. What's the point of correcting him? He'll only be confused. He is yet to fully understand—to comprehend— that he has a severe brain injury.

I force a smile. "Sounds like fun, David. Stuart's a great guy."

Lois bustles in to the rescue. "David, Rachel and I are going to talk in the other room."

"You can stay in here," the case manager says. "David, do you need to use the bathroom before lunch?" She ushers David out, not waiting for his answer, knowing it could be a long time coming.

Lois settles into an armchair. "How are you doing? Hannah and Joshie OK?"

"Actually, we're pretty good. Relatively speaking. They like their teachers. Joshie is doing well at the school, thank God. And I'm gaining weight, see?" I pat my thighs.

Approval is clear on Lois' face. "I'm glad. You look so much better."

"Yeah. I feel better. But I've been thinking a lot, talking with my therapist. I'm not ready to bring David home yet. Maybe after the first of the year . . .?"

Lois presses her lips together, shakes her head. "I don't recommend it. Once you take him home, it will be very hard to get him back into the rehab system. He's not likely to improve much in just a few months."

New information. I try to process the implication: either bring him home now for an indefinite amount of time or . . . never.

"So . . . what do you suggest?"

"Medically, David is more stable. But he isn't ready to leave here yet. If he stays seizure-free, we can consider moving him to Learning Services in January or early February."

From one institution to another. At least he'd be closer. My decision is still looming large, but less frightening than it's been.

What exactly am I afraid of? The disapproval of my community?
That I'll never move past the guilt?
What I'm afraid of is telling Dora.

. —.—. — . —.

She arrives in time for Chanukah. We invite Noam and his kids to our house. A perfectly innocent group of friends and family, lighting candles and feasting on Dora's delicious crispy latkes covered with my chunky homemade applesauce.

I won't tell her yet.

I find a great price on a rental cabin just outside of Yosemite. Dora is reluctant to be any distance from David, but I persuade her that the kids want to go to the snow—and they need a vacation. We'll visit David en route and on the way back.

If I tell her that it's really *me* who needs to get away, it wouldn't have had the same pull. I've figured out that—according to the rest of the world—my needs are far less important than the kids' or David's. I'm a Mother and a Wife. Now I'm a Mother and a Caregiver.

Rachel the Woman is disappearing.

. —.—. — . —.

I'm exhausted after a long day of playing in the snow with the kids, but I've been procrastinating the Big Reveal. Crawling into bed with their warm, non-judgmental little bodies is far more appealing than the task at hand, but I force myself to leave the bedroom after our bedtime story. Closing the door to their room, I stifle a yawn that escapes despite my apprehension.

"I think they're almost asleep, thank God."

Dora looks up. She's on the couch with a Hebrew novel open on her afghan-covered lap and a mug of chamomile tea. I've almost never seen Dora rest. She's an Israeli version of the Energizer Bunny. Mother of the year. Model wife. And nice, so nice.

"Oh good. They're tired from sledding."

Just go. Get it over with. I take a few steps toward the living room, but instead of sitting next to her and launching into my prepared speech, I wander to the fireplace and stare into it. A log falls. Sparks. A lovely crackling sound. I needlessly poke the burning wood around. I've imagined this scenario a thousand times, rehearsed my lines endlessly. The fire is vibrant, but the sweet smoky odor isn't comforting. *Give me strength, fire gods. Hell, I'll take any god out there who can hear me. Please, give me strength.*

I can feel Dora's eyes on my back. *Can she know what I'm about to say?*

You can do this, Rachel. Get over your spineless self. I drag myself away from the fire to find a comfortable position on the couch opposite her. "It's so nice here."

Dora picks up her mug of tea, studies it. "You're not going to bring him home, are you?"

Oh my God, has Tammy said something after all? I shake that off. The Conversation is happening. *Thank you, Dora. Thank you for saying what I couldn't say.*

She's staring at me. I can't decipher her expression. Disapproval? Accusation? No. Anger? No, definitely not.

"Dora, I'm so sorry." She's spared me saying the words. Even in that she is efficient. "I can't do it. I'm not like you. I don't have the strength to manage him and the children."

She is crying. I'm afraid if I stop talking the silence will kill me. I take a big swig of chardonnay.

"Lois and the other doctors say that I'll be a wreck if he comes home. That the family would fall apart from the stress. I'll get sick again, and what will happen to the kids?"

I'm a little ashamed of the trump cards that have landed in my lap. Abdicating duty. Exploiting doctor's orders. Using the children as an excuse. Pretty low on the self-actualizing, accepting-responsibility-for-your-actions scale.

I don't say that I haven't been in love with David. That our marriage was in such trouble when the accident happened that I'd fallen for someone else.

I want her to understand how hard this is. That I'm really not a selfish monster. But that would be focusing attention on my struggles, my fears of loss of freedom and independence—not on David's well-being, David's happiness. I want Dora's approval. Badly.

Dora's face is in her hands and her shoulders are shaking. Her sobs are quiet, puppy-like. This is worse, in a way, than if she had been shrieking, "You selfish, uncaring bitch. How could you abandon your husband? What's wrong with you? Do your fucking duty! You made a vow—in sickness and in health! How would you feel if it were *you* stuck away in an institution? How can you do this to him? To our whole family?"

No shrieking, no anger, no accusations. Only unbearable little soft cries.

I take another big swallow. "I'd need to hire someone to help. I have to work, and where would we put a caregiver? Our house is so small."

I've gone too far. She looks up. This time her look is fully decipherable. Disbelief. Sorrow. Deep, visceral, raw sorrow.

She doesn't have to say it. I can hear her accusation inside my head: *"Seriously? That's what you're worried about? That you have a fucking small house? Minor details. Logistics can be worked out. David needs to be home with his family! Not with strangers!"*

My dry eyes connect with her wet ones. My throat tightens, tears well up. This time I welcome them. *See, Dora, I am human. I am compassionate. I care.*

She shakes her head as if to say: *"I knew it. I saw the signs. For eight months he's been in institutions with no hint that you're preparing to bring him home."*

She asks, "Where will he go? What will happen to him?"

I rehearsed this part, too. "When he improves enough to leave NCS, I'm looking at Learning Services in Gilroy. It's a nice place, in the country. They have some cats. David likes cats."

Cats? Who the fuck am I kidding?

Pathetic. I try again. "It's only a half hour away. I can bring the kids to visit him at least once a week."

No response. We both need tissues. I have no idea where they keep Kleenex in this cabin. I go into the bathroom to get some toilet paper, legs shaking. She takes it without looking at me.

I stand behind her for a moment and stare at the dwindling fire. I should put another log on, but I can't move. I want to sit next to Dora, hold her tight, rocking and weeping together in sweet sharing. Forgiving and forgiven.

What if she casts off my arms? Rejects me?

Despite living on different continents, she's been such a good friend. We've taken long walks, talking, sharing secrets. She's sent her children to stay with us for weeks, months at a time. We've had a bond that—as I'd been told by friends—is rare with an in-law. Sometimes I've thought I liked Dora better than David—which always embarrasses me. I don't want to lose that.

I already have.

Another log falls with a loud crack. I flinch and shuffle back to my spot on the couch, curling into a ball. Dora gazes at her novel, which has fallen to the floor. On our separate perches, in that mountain cabin, we are both quiet. I swirl the tablespoon of remaining wine in the smudged glass, nauseated by its stale alcoholic odor. I start to say something, anything. *You're not mad? You still love me, right? Thanks for not yelling at me?*

"I'm sorry, Dora. I'm so, so sorry."

We sit in silence for a long time, watching the fire die.

Chapter 12

IN JANUARY I HELP LOIS AND NICKI, his case manager, settle David in at Learning Services. Lois, my hero as usual, had fought for a private room. Again the furniture is outdated—twin bed with a rust/brown polyester plaid bedspread. I make a mental note to replace it. I put a happy-family photo on the dresser, the four of us on a ski trip. Is it fair to display a lie? True in the past, but a more honest picture would have a jagged tear separating David from the three of us.

Add that to the list. The list of things-Rachel-feels-guilty-about. I hadn't caused the brain injury—but I was perpetuating the rift.

Yes, I've told Dora. But telling David he wouldn't be coming home? Unimaginable. I channel Scarlett O'Hara—I'll think about it tomorrow. There will be plenty of tomorrows.

Nancy says I should ask myself what I *can* do for David—and not beat myself up over what I can't. The family can visit David at Learning Services at least once a week. He can also come to the house to spend time with us in San Jose. Weekends—when structured activities at Learning Services are minimal—are best. The kids are young enough to go along with my agenda, so off we go every Sunday afternoon.

The live-in residents include Kurt, a thin, vacant-eyed man who could be anyone's elder uncle or grandpa. He's always at the dining room table carefully folding cloth napkins—stacks and stacks. There's blind Angie who likes to help us navigate the place ("I think David is in the TV room—let me show you where it is.") Pedro is short and heavyset, with a dark Burt Reynolds-style mustache. He's been in a motorcycle crash. "*Hola!*" he bellows as we sit waiting for David to finish his snack, emphasizing the final words of every sentence. "You are very pretty! Are you David's wife? Are those David's children? The children are beautiful! You are beautiful! How long are you staying? How long is David staying? I'm leaving tomorrow! Going to pack my suitcase now!"

"That's great, Pedro!" I say brightly. It's clear Pedro isn't going anywhere.

Nicki tells me that some of the residents are there voluntarily, and some—like David—are placed there by family members. Others simply have nowhere else to go.

David doesn't belong. He has a masters in electrical engineering, a well-paying high tech job, owns a home. Though I don't know their backstories, I assume most of the residents—compared to David—are under-educated, uncultured. I don't like seeing David among them. I'm a TBI snob. *Add it to the list.*

Amazing how we establish our status everywhere we find ourselves.

Who does belong in a place like that? It's like finding out you have cancer—suddenly you're part of a club you never wanted to join.

Though I know they are harmless, I worry about the kids' exposure to some of the residents. But as parents, don't we want to teach our kids tolerance, to foster sensitivity and compassion?

When Hannah was in kindergarten, her school had several special needs classes. One morning she saw the students in wheelchairs being lowered from the minibus.

"Look at that boy," she said loudly. "Why is he acting so funny?"

"Sshh, honey. I'll tell you later. Don't point." I glance in his direction and smile apologetically, as if to say *I'm sorry if you heard that. She didn't mean it. She's only five. I promise to teach her not to stare and point. I promise to teach her to respect you, to be kind, to be tolerant.*

On the drive home that day, I try. "Honey, those kids may look or act differently than other kids, but they have feelings. Their brains or bodies just don't work like ours. We need to treat them nicely, OK?"

"OK, Mommy." In the rearview mirror I see Hannah in her booster seat, curling her hair around her finger and staring out the car window. "When I get home can I put on my Sleeping Beauty dress?"

So much for a teachable moment.

Many of the residents' therapies are held in the Learning Services recreation room. It houses a Foosball table, stair-stepper, treadmill, and a few bookcases stocked with worn board games, blocks, and packs of playing cards. At first the kids are excited. They especially love the most dangerous piece of equipment, the treadmill. Despite my vehement protests, they turn it up to the highest speed, screeching as they try to keep up with the fast-moving belt. But even that glamour wears off pretty quickly. After a few weeks they start resisting the visits—they're bored, they whine.

Coming up with activities for the four of us is a colossal challenge. There is an outlet mall nearby. A trip to Best Buy for a charging cable or Target for socks becomes an afternoons' entertainment. We are regulars at the local Chinese and frozen yogurt places.

I meet someone at the JCC gym who knows a woman who does equestrian therapy in nearby Morgan Hill. Great, horseback riding! What's not to like? It will be expensive but probably a big hit with the kids. And David used to enjoy riding—we'd gone a few times as a family. I make the arrangements.

The scents of manure, hay, and horse sweat mingle in the unseasonable heat of late March. Martha, the therapist, comes out to greet us. "Hello and welcome!"

Hannah is bursting with excitement. "Mommy, can I see the horses now?"

I look at Martha.

"Sure," she says. "You can help me get them ready for our session."

"C'mon, Joshie, let's go!" She runs off in the direction Martha pointed.

Joshie sprints after her. "I want a spotted one!"

I help David out of the car. He moves with excruciating deliberateness—and with great trepidation—in the unfamiliar setting.

"Do you work with brain injuries often?" I ask Martha as we follow the kids. We are making our way down the path to the stable.

"Not so much," she says. "Mostly autistic and Down syndrome children, or kids with other severe cognitive disabilities."

I think about Joshie's Asperger's—this could be good for him, too, more than just entertainment. *Slow down, Rachel. One thing at a time.*

Martha is observing David's cautious gait, his fragility, his misshapen, creviced face and forehead. "Did you bring a doctor's note?"

Oh no. "I didn't know we needed one." Martha and I had spoken briefly on the phone, but apparently one of us didn't ask the right questions.

"Well," she said, "I thought he'd be alright with the helmet, but I didn't realize the extent of his injuries. If there's any kind of fall, it could be very bad." Translation: she'd be liable. *Right. Of course. I should have known he would need an authorization. Am I ever going to get this right?*

"Well, David can watch the kids ride, right? I can work on getting the authorization and he can ride next time."

"Sure, sounds good." Martha pulls saddles out of a tack closet. "C'mon guys, help me with the bridles!"

Another disappointment. I take a deep breath and explain to David that he won't be able to ride today.

"It's fucking hot out here," he responds.

When the horses are ready, Martha shows the kids how to lead them by the reins toward the corral. Thankfully it's covered, but even in the shade the corral is like an oven. David and I sit in an observation area, separated from the main corral by a low barrier wall. Martha starts with Hannah, showing her the basics of sitting in the saddle, how to use the reins. Joshie, not a paragon of patience as usual, is having a hard time waiting his turn. Satisfied that Hannah is trotting capably, Martha helps Joshie up on the horse and soon has him trotting, too.

David intently stares at Joshie, motionless. Despite the heat, dust, and smell I'm calm, relieved that for a little while at least everyone seems happy and occupied. Things hadn't gone exactly according to plan, but then when had they? Plan B seems to be my new normal.

"How old was he when we adopted him?" David's question interrupts my musing.

"What?"

"Him." David points at Joshie. "The boy. How old was he when we adopted him?"

My husband, our kids' father, the one who had gripped my hand and encouraged me while I pushed our baby out into the world, doesn't remember the pregnancy, the birth, that he fathered this child.

Why am I still surprised at such moments?

Of course I know—intellectually—that it isn't simply a memory lapse. David's tattered brain can't make the connection. He knows there's some relationship with this child, that he's been involved in raising him. But he doesn't understand how this blond boy on the trotting horse had gotten here, nor where he came from. There are simply too many gaps. He can't connect the dots.

I close my eyes against the welling tears and force myself to take yet another deep breath. Then another.

"He's our son, David. Yours and mine. I gave birth to him seven years ago."

David narrows his eyes in confusion.

I wipe some sweat off my neck. "Joshie was born on January 28th, 1999, at the Los Gatos Community Hospital, at around four in the afternoon. You had a cold so they made you wear a mask. Remember?" *Remember. What a stupid question.*

David is studying Joshie—who's giggling with delight as he trots. "Look Mommy!" *Why doesn't he want David to look, too? Have they written David off as their parent? Am I overthinking?*

David still doesn't make the connection that Joshie is his son. But he's accepting my story as the truth. That is a victory.

· — ·· — · — — ·

I think I've done my penance by suffering the consequences of my affair with Mark. Diane, apparently, thinks differently. I'd heard that they are back together, but she won't leave me alone.

Shortly after I'd ended the relationship the previous summer, Diane began calling the house. At first she just hung up. Later she became bolder. "Hello, is zere a Mr. Mark Berman zere? I vas tolt he vould be zere."

It was the worst German accent I'd ever heard, a female voice trying to sound male. So pathetic I almost laughed out loud the first time. But as soon as I'd hung up I started to shake. Diane really is a nutcase. Assuming an accent—who *does* that? I told her I won't see him again, and I haven't. I'm doing something right. Can't she punish her husband instead of me? I hadn't yet invoked the word *stalker*, but it was feeling that way, though I'm rarely afraid. But I took some satisfaction that Mark was suffering, too. Or is he? Did he even know that she's calling me? Was she really looking for him? What does it say about me, that I'd fallen for someone who could willingly return to a relationship with a possessive lunatic?

Eventually the calls dwindle. She seemed to have let it go.

A few months after the phone calls, I found a large nail in my car tire. Probably construction somewhere in the neighborhood. Bad luck, it can happen to anyone. A few days later, strike two, discovered in my driveway. A merely unfortunate (expensive) coincidence. The following week, strike three. This was no coincidence. This was sinister, calculated. Retaliation carefully planned.

Five months later I learn just how sinister she could be.

The kids and I are returning from a spring break road trip to Palm Springs for Passover with friends, Legoland, and LA to visit my cousin. I'm proud—elated even—that I've somehow managed to organize a normal vacation despite the chaos that is our existence. But eight hours of are-we-there-yet, he's-kicking-me, and she-did-it-first have served to turn a mild headache into a jackhammer that's pounding my forehead. I'm hungry, my back aches, and I dread the inevitable battle that will ensue when I try to get them to help unload the car and unpack.

Crankiness turns to relief as we finally turn down our tree-lined street. I love April, with the sycamores leafing out, the lime green brilliant and fresh. Promising renewal. Another chance.

Hannah interrupts my reverie as we near the house. "Mommy, what's that on our grass?"

I don't see anything. As I pull into the driveway, all I can think is, thank God, we're home. I'm already hours in the future, envisioning a warm sudsy bath to revel in when the kids are in bed. I get out of the car. Then I see it.

"Look Mommy, look! There's gigantic letters in the grass!" Joshie triumphantly spells them out for me. "W—H—O—R—E." He looks at me quizzically. "What's a wa-ho-ree?"

Holy shit.

"It's nothing, buddy," I hear myself saying automatically. *God fucking damn it. God fucking damn her.*

The capital letters are clear, unmistakable. Each letter is three feet tall and two feet wide. WHORE. They've been burned into the grass with some kind of solvent—bleach, most likely, or lighter fluid—with an eerie accuracy, as if a giant template has been carefully laid down to form each perfect curve and straighten every line. Calculated, planned.

Strike four.

"Mommy, are you OK?" I hear Hannah ask as if from far away. My darling girl, ever the caretaker.

"Joshie, get away from there!" I yell. He's on the H, carefully walking the letters, as if they are a balance beam.

Joshie dashes toward the house. Trembling, I unlock the front door for him.

Our neighbor Ron appears, as if from nowhere, a grim look clouding his eyes.

"It's been there since this morning." He's wringing his hands as if to apologize. "Probably happened during the night."

I shoot him a desperate glance.

"What happened, mommy?" Hannah persists. "What is whore? Is it bad?" She sees my—and Ron's—distress. Her lower lip trembles. "I'm scared."

What. The. Fuck. This can't be happening.

Ron—dear, Jehovah's Witness, childless Ron—smiles at Hannah. "I'll bet it was some boys playing a mean prank. It happens all the time around here." Suddenly I love Ron with all my heart.

"Yes, honey, it was just a joke. Some bad boys."

Hannah looks worried, but runs after Joshie, forgetting—as I have—about helping with the suitcases.

Ron smiles again, this time at me. "I'll take care of it tomorrow. I'll hire some guys, some day laborers. I'll have them take it out and lay down new sod."

He pauses, and in that pause I flush with shame. What had a moment before been shock, then cover-up, then strategizing, has become humiliation.

I force myself to look at the gigantic, vicious word smack in the center of my tidy, well-fertilized lawn, announcing to my children, my neighborhood, the world, that the woman who lives here is a slut, a home wrecker, a bitch. An unfit mother.

Ron has the lawn repaired the next morning. After a few weeks it's almost impossible to see where the letters had been. We fall back into our routine. Get the kids to school. Referee their fights. Decide what to make for dinner. Laundry, book reports, fractions.

But for a long time before going to bed Hannah insists on closing her windows tight against the bad guys, even on the hottest nights.

. —.—. — —.

After finally crawling out of survival mode, I'm flung back into it. Diane's nighttime escapade pushes me to the edge. Naked. Exposed. Our house is no longer a haven of safety and continuity. I watch my appetite shrink again. I'm frightened. *I fought so hard to get over that eating disorder. I can't go back there.*

I consult an attorney friend about a restraining order but we have no proof. He suggests a security camera. The cost is overwhelming. I can only hope that the lawn incident is Diane's grand finale.

Chapter 13

JOSH'S SCHOOL JOURNAL—APRIL 24, 2006
On April 14th I lost my second top front tooth! I couldn't
eat and talk so well so I just ate with my back side teeth.
It was easier to eat cotton candy. It was hardist to eat
gummy bears. I really like my two top front teeth lost.
And I'm about to loose one bottom tooth.

Dora is reluctantly coming to terms with the reality (not accept—
she'll never accept) that I'm unwilling to assume the caregiver
role. But she's on a mission to get David out of Learning Services. The very least I should do is to move him into an apartment
near us and hire people to care for him. I explain—repeatedly—
that I'm advised to wait until the lawsuit is settled. The cost to
house and care for David—around $20,000 a month—might
bankrupt us before any settlement can be reached.

"If you think it's hard now," Dr. Winegardner at Learning
Services says when I propose the idea, "just wait until you're
trying to manage his apartment, his daily needs, his rehab—and

especially caregivers—by yourself. It's impossibly hard to find trained, reliable people. And keep them."

Dora has inspired my cynicism. *You just don't want to lose the $16,000 you're getting from worker's comp every month.*

True statements, both. But my allegiance tilts toward the doctor. I don't have the stamina. Not to care for David at home, nor anywhere else. Not to continue to love him. Not to be a wife. I can barely go to the grocery store without breaking down, overwhelmed by the choices.

I tell Dora that Nicki, Dr. Winegardner, Mike the attorney, and Lois are against it. Dora is sure they're all in cahoots. Learning Services gets a well-paying client, Lois and Mike get to stay in control.

I am in the middle, trying to keep everyone happy.

"You can use your savings," Dora says. "It's David's money, too."

"Dora, please. I know. But the lawsuit could take years. We don't have that kind of savings."

Across the 7,000 miles I can feel her accusation: You have the power, Rachel. You're not bringing him home, OK, but you can get him out of there, put him in an apartment. Anywhere else, just not in an institution. "Let him come to Israel. I'll take care of him."

I sigh. "Dora, I've told you. We need to wait for the lawsuit to settle out."

She's silent. She knows this is true. Still, she grows fiercer in her mission: to fight the system and me—the jailor. To release the innocent prisoner.

. — .— . — —.

I had met Gabi when we lived in Munich in the winter of 1997.

David had arranged a six-month work trade with another marketing guy at Siemens. We would spend some time with

David's family and friends; I could practice my German and experience living in a cosmopolitan European city. David's mother Maria was beside herself with the prospect of some quality time with six-month-old Hannah. I took a much-needed leave of absence from my cantorial job at the temple and off we went to freeze in Munich.

We moved into the colleague's studio apartment in the center of the city—cramped but clean—above a delectable Turkish restaurant where we ordered lamb with yogurt sauce to eat in our tiny kitchen. While David was at work I would bundle Hannah into her fleece sack and we'd explore Munich. I mastered the fine art of getting on and off the S-Bahn with a stroller. Hannah loved to gnaw on soft pretzels I'd buy hot and fresh in the Marienplatz. Several times a week Maria happily took care of the baby while I attended a German class.

An array of David's childhood friends still lived in Munich. The city's Jewish community, almost entirely Holocaust survivors and their children and grandchildren, existed in a self-imposed isolation within their inherent distrust of the gentile world, the *goyim.* Jewish community buildings and synagogues were unmarked, protected by police—perpetuating a barrier between gentile and Jew.

Everyone wanted to meet me, David's new American wife. Jossi, David's closest friend from childhood, was successful as an attorney and a ladies' man. Robbie, a staunch defender of old-world Judaism, had three young children with his Israeli wife Vered (who sorely missed Israel and spoke German with a thick Hebrew accent). Danny and Maggie, about to have their first baby, were full of questions for us about caring for a newborn.

And Gabi. She was a freelance photographer who lived in the trendy Bohemian neighborhood of Schwabing. David reported she'd been carrying on a not-so-discreet affair for years with a married Frenchman in Marseille. She was dark-eyed and dark-haired in an attractive, tousled, artsy kind of way. Gabi offered to babysit so that David and I could go out to dinner with friends.

"Schmoofie!" she crooned to Hannah as she opened the door to her loft. "Give her to me!" Gabi snatched the baby out of her stroller and whisked her down the hall. I glanced at David. He just shrugged, as if to say, *Gabi's always like that.* The apartment looked like a movie set for funky free spirits. Gabi's own work covered every inch of wall space.

I stopped in front of a tasteful series of a male nude. "This is really good," I said. "Beautiful."

"*Ach, ja* . . . that was shot in Brussels. Yves was my lover for a few months." Gabi was nonchalant as she nuzzled her face into Hannah's milky-smelling hair. "Schmoofie! You are so *süss*, so *wunderschön*!" Hannah beamed a two-tooth grin and waved her chubby fists at Gabi's high-pitched compliments. "I will photograph you, Schmoofielein!"

David and I trailed along behind as Gabi strode around the loft with Hannah in her arms. "Here is a piece I did in Vienna, and these two were in a gallery in Berlin." She gestured with her head at a pair of stunning portraits of a young girl at play. "I leave for Marseille on Monday at six in the morning to set up an exhibition."

David raised his eyebrows at me. *That's not all she's doing in Marseille.*

I was a bit queasy with jealousy. The stark contrast in our lives was painfully apparent. At six in the morning on Monday, I'd be nursing and/or diapering a crying baby in a tiny studio apartment. Gabi's artistic and physical freedom from constraints pissed me off just a little.

Still, I liked her: wild, colorful, quirky. A little full of herself maybe. But isn't that the hallmark, the unspoken societal permission—expectation even—of an artist? A little narcissism goes a long way in the creative process, doesn't it?

When Joshie was born a year later, we received a card with an original photo on the back and Gabi's logo. "*Mazel tov!*" she'd written. "How's my schmoofie? Love, Gabi."

Then for seven years, no contact.

So I'm happy when I hear that Gabi will be coming with Dora on this visit. Gabi's lively eccentricity will cheer David up and keep Dora company during her stay. David's long-term memory is somewhat intact—they can relive Munich memories.

Gabi will be a great buffer between Dora and me. We're still on speaking terms, though the tension between us is increasingly intolerable. I invite them to Shabbat dinner the day after they arrive.

"My schmoofie is all grown up!" Gabi shrieks as Hannah opens the door. Hannah recoils, but Gabi sweeps in and enfolds her in a great hug. She spots Joshie over Hannah's shoulder. "And who's this? *Der kleiner David?* Little David? You look just like your papa when he was your age!"

We light the candles, sing the blessings, pass around the challah I'd picked up at Noah's Bagels that morning. After dinner the kids are excused and run off to watch something inane on the Disney channel—*That's So Raven*, *Hannah Montana*, or *The Suite Life of Zach and Cody*—fantasy worlds where all the kids are witty, the adults stupid, and every problem is resolved in half an hour.

Dora, Gabi, and I linger over coffee and ice cream. I'm eager to hear about Gabi's artistic endeavors of the past seven years. She's continued to show her work in galleries all over Europe, successfully supporting herself. This time I'm more impressed than jealous.

Gabi puts down her coffee cup. "I've been talking to David every day. You know he's miserable." She speaks matter-of-factly.

I glance at Dora. She doesn't meet my gaze. *Here we go.* I haven't been avoiding the topic. Not really. But I'm not about to bring it up.

Gabi folds her napkin with intense deliberateness. "He wants to leave. He hates it there. Do you know they won't let him smoke, even in his own room? Or leave if he wants to? And that they force him to do these childish exercise classes?"

"Hold on," I interrupt. Feebly—I haven't begun to prepare my defense. "I know it's not the best situation, but it's only temporary, until the lawsuit is settled." Beads of sweat are forming on my hairline. Instinctively I glance toward the TV room, grateful that Hannah Montana is drowning out the impending attack. Dora stirs her half-melted ice cream.

"It's torture for him," Gabi continues. "Do you know how smart David is? He says that the other inmates—that's what he calls them, *inmates*—are all idiots. He has no one to talk to. He's surrounded by lunatics."

Later I'll remember how calculated her tone, how manipulative her manner. But at that moment I run my hand through my hair, sip the lukewarm coffee. It matters to me that she knows I'm not evil or entirely selfish. I still want her to understand.

More importantly, I want Dora to understand.

Gabi leans forward, her dark eyes accusing. "How could you do this? How can you lock him away?" She settles back in her chair. Contented. "What kind of a wife does this to her husband?"

What the fuck? Who is she to tell me how to live my life, make my decisions? This is my dinner table, my house, my husband. Suddenly I don't give a shit how far she's travelled, how gorgeous her photographs, how good her intentions.

I speak quietly. "I think you need to leave." I'm surprised, but take courage from speaking my truth. With years of vocal training I know how to project my voice, command an audience of hundreds. I access my crescendo. "You need to leave. I don't have to take this."

Undaunted, Gabi continues her calm, deliberate tirade. "All of David's friends are disgusted with you. Do you like being a jailor? Are you in love with having so much power?"

Dora is studying her ice cream. *Is that true? Do they hate me? Jossi, Robbie, Vered? Even Maggie and Danny?*

I stand up. "You need to leave now. I won't be treated this way in my own home. You're no longer welcome here."

Poor Dora looks miserable. Screw that—damn her for putting me in this position. I will not turn into the bitch they already think I am.

Dora seems to gather her courage, almost knocking the chair over as she leaps up. "I'll do the dishes." The plates clank as she frantically stacks them. Gabi is still leaning back in her chair— my chair—an odd look of triumph in those dark eyes.

"Dora." I say, gently. I put my hand on her arm. "I'll take care of the dishes. Please take Gabi back to the hotel."

For the first time since David's accident, I feel clear. Justified. Leonine.

But after they've gone, I sit. Watch the Shabbat candles dwindle, undistracted by dirty dishes. Shaking.

· — · — · — · ·

I have no plans to go to the bank. I made a deposit the day before; the checks I just gotten from my morning students could wait. But the early summer sky is bright and clean, the air pure and promising, a welcome escape from the morass of Gabi malice.

As I walk down sycamore-lined Meredith Avenue I smile at a gardener. He politely turns off the deafening roar of his leaf-blower as I pass. *It isn't his fault that landscape maintenance has become so strident, so annoying. He's just doing his job.*

"Hi." My slight nod says, *thanks for turning that damn thing off.*

He looks slightly embarrassed. They always do. "*Hola,*" he says, and goes back to work.

The blower whirrs. *E-flat. Fortissimo.* The music of the afternoon in San Jose.

I turn right on Lincoln and cross the street. Living two blocks away from Willow Glen, our mini-downtown neighborhood within sprawling San Jose, delights me. I love walking over for a manicure, taking the kids for frozen yogurt, picking up toothpaste or Chinese takeout. I can do errands, get exercise, and reduce my carbon footprint all at the same time.

Usually I don't go into the bank. The ATMs work fine for almost everything. I have no idea why I'm entering.

"Good afternoon!" says the smiling "concierge" who hovers near the teller line—like a hotel but without so many fun events to offer (deposit? withdrawal? safe deposit box?). "How are you today?" Automatic.

"Fine, thanks." Automatic. Less enthusiasm than I'd shown to the gardener.

Then I think I might be hallucinating. I see Gabi and Dora, with David between them. At the desk of an attractive, business-suited woman. *Christina Flores*, says the nameplate. I don't know how I read that name while the floor is falling away.

"What the hell are you doing here?" A rhetorical question—I know exactly what they're doing. Trying to withdraw money from my account. Mine and David's.

I glare at Gabi. *You bitch. You. Fucking. Bitch.*

David and I have investment accounts at Charles Schwab, but I'd recently moved $30,000 into our Wells Fargo account for legal fees and continually mounting living expenses. And I gave

Dora $10,000 to help with her travel. I picture Gabi gleefully grinning as—with Dora's assistance and permission—she takes control over our money, our house, our lives.

No! My scream is silent.

I manage to wobble the few steps toward them.

Dora's head shoots up. She's been looking at her hands in her lap, fiddling with her purse straps. Her eyes widen with disbelief. "*Um Gottes willen, nein.* Oh my God, oh no," she moans, burying her face in her hands.

Gabi doesn't flinch. "*Es macht nichts,*" she says to no one in particular. "It doesn't matter. *WIR haben rechts.* We're right."

Gabi has *chutzpah.*

I could kill her.

"There's my wife," David says happily.

I want to comfort him. Reassure him that he'll be protected. But he's flanked by a different team. I'm the opposition now.

"Are you Mrs. Michelberg?" Christina stands. *She knows.*

"I'm Rachel Michelberg," I announce, falling back on my theatrical training. *Help me,* my eyes plead. *Protect me. Protect David from this vampire. Be on my team. I'm the right side, the good side.*

I don't know how Christina manages to assess the situation so quickly, so accurately. It doesn't matter. She does.

Gabi won't meet my stare, so I glare at the top of Dora's head. She's crumpled, one arm wrapped around her waist, her forehead cradled in the other hand—rubbing her eyes as if trying to wipe me out of reality. Or am I seeing shame?

Christina gathers up a few papers from her desk, strides toward me. "I think it's better if we talk in private." She glances back at the two women. "Will you excuse us for a moment?" Not waiting for an answer, she gently takes my elbow and steers me toward the lobby area.

This has to be illegal. Maybe I'll sue her. Wouldn't that be fun!
Nah, too many lawsuits—and lawyers—in my life already.

"Here, sit down." Christina gestures. "I understand what's happening, and I think I know what we can do to prevent it. Do you have an account here in your name only?"

"I don't think so. I used to." I was fine with David handling the financials. We hadn't had personal accounts since we got married.

"That's not a problem. We can open one right now, and I'll move most of the funds from your joint account into the new individual account. They won't be able to withdraw those funds then."

"You can do that?" Stammering in my gratitude, it doesn't occur to me to ask if that's legal, let alone ethical. "Oh my God, thank you so much."

"Yes, I'll take care of it. You stay here and I'll tell them there's nothing I can do. They're not going to like it, but it's a good temporary fix."

Christina is clearly vying with Lois for sainthood. I picture the two of them with white gossamer gowns and angel's wings, hovering over me with open arms, crooning words of comfort, promising eternal protection. Maybe it had been Christina who'd whispered in my ear: *Go to the bank. Bad things will happen if you don't go. You need to be there. Now.*

I wait in the lobby, forcing myself to slow my breathing, while my angel Christina informs the trio that she can't help them today. My eyes are glued to my lap, so I don't see what happens next. I imagine Gabi arguing with Christina then striding out. I imagine Dora helping a bewildered David to his feet, murmuring soothing words that he can't possibly comprehend. I wonder if—despite his corrupted brain—he feels emasculated by these willful women fighting to control him.

I'm sorry, David. But we won this time. This really is the best strategy. I promise I'll keep defending us.

But the episode chips away at my fragile new confidence.

· —·—·— ·—·

Gabi is on a mission. In the guise of Dora's crusader and David's savior, she becomes my tormentor.

Since Dora timed her visit for David's birthday, it's the occasion to throw the Polynesian party he always wanted. The kids and I shop at Costco for tiki torches and pineapple. We have fun designing and ordering a big cake. I hire a former student to perform a hula dance.

"Gabi isn't invited," I tell Dora firmly. After the shit Gabi has been pulling I don't want her anywhere near me or my house. Not that I'm not pissed at Dora for the whole bank debacle. But a part of me understands. She's desperate to help David, to improve his living situation, and she reached out for help. I actually admire her resourcefulness.

But I'm feeling proprietary about this party. For a change I'm doing something to make David—our whole family—happy.

A lovely June day. How much has changed since a year ago when I was writhing in agony on our sofa, my insides tattered and torn, as David was about to come home for good.

The yard is filled with laughter. Joshie darts about in his Hawaiian shirt; my friends mix margaritas (not exactly Polynesian, but close enough for California). Izz's ukulele version of *Somewhere Over the Rainbow* plays on what seems like a continuous loop.

"Where's Daddy?" Hannah asks, placing tiny umbrellas on drinks with her friend Cassandra.

"Aunt Dora is bringing him from Learning Services." Slicing pineapple, I glance at the clock. "He should be here by now."

From the sink I have a clear shot of the street and driveway. As if on cue, Gabi is striding down the driveway like a fucking queen, carrying a cake box. Dora and David, her entourage, trail behind.

"Schmoofie! Joshie! Look who's here! I've brought your Daddy and his birthday cake!"

What the holy fuck.

I want to scratch her eyes out.

It's just a cake. Why such a big deal? In these days fraught with doubt, uncertainty, and guilt, the smallest act is magnified to a crushing degree.

The kids run out to greet David. Girlfriends who'd been helping me in the kitchen gather around me, cooing words of support—Sue, Karen, Jacie. They all know the Gabi story. "You've got this, don't let her ruin this for you, remember this is your house, your family."

Surrounded by reinforcements, trying to hold my head up, I head to the backyard. Gabi is already holding court, her cake placed prominently in the center of the table, ours pushed aside.

Brava, Gabi. Well done. You're now the star, the center of attention, David's savior.

"Ignore her," Sue whispers. "Don't give her the satisfaction."

She's right. It's just a stupid cake. Get over it.

I talk, I clean, I serve food. Occasionally I throw Gabi a dirty look which she ignores. I applaud the hula dancers. We light the tiki torches. David is clearly happy.

I'm embarrassed to realize that I'm deep in self-pity. I worked so hard to put this party together. Was it just to show everyone—especially myself—that I still care about David? That I really am willing to put myself out for him?

Lose-lose. *Stop beating yourself up. You're doing what you can.*

It never seems enough.

Chapter 14

WITH DORA AND GABI GONE I think our household can
find some new normal. But I forgot about Diane—until the
morning there's a badly lettered cardboard sign balanced on my
rear car window.

I don't have to read more than two words to realize that
it's obscene.

"What's that, Mommy?" Hannah aware and curious, as I
snatch the sign, its back toward her.

"Just some kind of advertisement." My heart is pounding.
"Get in the car." I run back in the house, fumble with the
keys, and stash it in a closet. *Please let Hannah not ask any more
questions. Please let this not increase her anxiety. Please, Diane, leave
us the fuck alone.*

Later that day a neighbor knocks on our door. He and his
wife had seen someone put the sign on our car, at around mid-
night. A red-haired woman. She'd parked across the street next
to his house, put on a trench coat and sunglasses before glancing
around and carefully placing the sign on the car. They're willing
to make a statement that they'd witnessed the incident.

Sunglasses? Was this some cheesy film noir plot?

Now with the sign and the witness, I have proof. I can get a restraining order. She won't be allowed within a hundred feet of me, the house, the kids. No contact. Even so, it feels humiliating, sleazy, trashy. Nice Jewish girls shouldn't need restraining orders. Especially from a middle-aged female.

But even with legal protection, I'll only feel a little safer. She's still out there. And now the legal intervention will fuel her hatred. Who knows when she might strike again?

And where the fuck is Mark in all this?

. ----- -- -.

This summer I am teaching a theater camp, picking up a few cantorial jobs, and building a voice studio. Support from Passavé has ended. Aside from Social Security, there's no regular income. We may eventually have a windfall from the lawsuit, but nothing is certain. Meanwhile, I have to build a new career. Luckily I've been in the music community for a long time. I have a piano, lots of sheet music, a nice living room space for teaching. Voice students begin to fill my schedule.

Mike advises me—again—to be patient with the lawsuit. He and his partner Kristine are working hard on the information and evidence gathering—"discovery"— phase. They believe that the sealant used by the maintenance facility in Reno was probably the culprit.

"But you said the Reno guys don't have any assets."

"Right. But Teledyne Continental is a huge company. They make the Gasket Maker sealant and the engine parts. They're conceding that the sealant did cause the engine to come apart in flight, but they're suggesting the mechanic in Reno should not have used that product. We're planning to argue that Teledyne's instruction manual isn't clear about which sealant to use and which to avoid." Mike's voice over the phone is positively giddy. "And believe me, Teledyne has assets."

I'm quiet. I hate the deep pockets thing. But if it will provide financial security for David, for us? Money means freedom. Money means options. I shouldn't feel sorry for Teledyne—they'll be fine.

"Rachel? You still there?"

"I'm here."

"I think we have a good case."

I try not to get too excited. I've learned that hoping for the best and expecting the worst is, unfortunately, a good motto.

Kristine, Mike's partner, calls a few weeks later. "I know this is a tough question, but we need to know if you're planning to stay married to David. It's critical to how we structure the case regarding the economic needs of your family. We don't need to worry about this for a while, but it will be coming up."

Jesus.

Of course I'd been thinking about divorce. It's a constant topic in therapy and conversations with friends. I'm only forty-four and still alive Down There. But divorce is terrifying. David and the kids will—theoretically—be supported, assuming there's some kind of financial award. But what about me? Will I be persona non grata?

I'm embarrassed. But I'm learning how to look after myself. "And me?"

"You can sue for Loss of Consortium—the loss of companionship of a loved one. There will be a dollar amount we will ask for," Kristine says. "It will be a fraction of what you would get if you remain married, but it could still be significant."

"If I admit I want a divorce, do I retain rights to make decisions about David?"

"No, that would be considered a conflict of interest. Normally we'd think about someone else in the family taking over, but with Dora and Sigi so far away—and they're clearly not being practical about the legal implications of his care right now—Mike and I absolutely don't recommend it. You should think about a court-appointed conservator to make financial and treatment decisions."

A conservator. An impartial stranger. *Hmm. It would get me off the hook.*

I have to decide if I'm going to stay married to David and remain his guardian ad litem, his decision maker.

If I do:
- Chances are that the kids and I would be set for life.
- I would be a hero. "She is so strong," everyone would say.
- It would be for the appearance and the financial security.

But if I do:
- At what emotional price?
- Staying married would be a lie.

The answer is clear. I have to be honest. It's the least I can do for David.

There will be a divorce.

Whenever I ask, Learning Services brings David home to San Jose. Sometimes friends join us, especially Karen and Alex whose children are close to Hannah and Joshie. We sit in the backyard, drink wine, watch the kids on the play structure that David assembled when he could still follow instructions safely. Sometimes Alex takes David inside ostensibly to play video games, but

Karen and I know they're going out front to smoke cigarettes. We shoot hoops or try to play ping-pong. David is agitated when he misses the ball—and when the kids misbehave, which is frequently.

David is particularly impatient with his son. Joshie's repetitive behaviors irritate him.

"Look! Watch me going down the slide!" Joshie calls for the tenth (or twentieth) time. He constantly craves adult attention.

"I don't care," David yells back.

Joshie looks stricken. He runs into the house, not wanting the other kids to see the tears streaming down his face.

"David, you need to be nicer to your son," I admonish—as if it will make a difference. I head after Joshie—he'll be tough to console. I can't remember if David was harder on Joshie than Hannah before the accident. Most fathers do have higher standards for their sons. But David's unfiltered put-downs are devastating.

I find him on his bed, face buried in his pillow. "Why is Daddy so nasty?" he whimpers.

I sit down next to him and stroke his back. "Daddy doesn't mean it that way. Remember what I told you? His brain just doesn't know how to be nice sometimes." Joshie turns over to look at me, sniffles. I wipe some tears from his cheek with my thumb. "He really loves you."

From the look on Joshie's face, I'm not sure he believes me.

- — -·— -— — -·

One evening when I'm slicing tomatoes for our dinner salad, I notice that that the car is not in the driveway.

"Where's Daddy?" I ask Joshie, smiling too brightly. *Hide the fear.*

"Dunno. I think he drove somewhere," Joshie says, carefully arranging his new obsession—Pokémon cards—on the floor.

"David?" I call. No answer. I run to my purse. The car keys are gone. *Fuck.* I dash into the street. Thank God our Nissan Murano is parked at the curb a few driveways down. Joe from next door is talking with David who is in the driver's seat.

"David says he wants to go play pool with Stuart." Joe is trying to pretend that it's normal for a brain-injured man to drive around the neighborhood.

"Thanks, Joe." I give him one of those grateful forced smiles I've perfected, the one that also says, *"This really sucks, doesn't it?"* "Hey David, slide over. I'll drive us home and you can help me wash lettuce."

David doesn't resist. He grimaces as he slides into the passenger seat. The shattered vertebrae in his low back still cause him constant pain.

I catch Joe's look of pity as he watches me make the U-turn back to our house.

. — .— . — — .

Gabi's words—*"all of David's friends in Germany are disgusted with you"*—haunt me. As crazy as she is, I sense that there's truth in them. She's been giving them an earful. Even normally complacent Sigi and his wife Tina are certainly grumbling about me locking David away in a loony bin.

They're making me out to be Cruella de Ville. They see their childhood friend powerless, imprisoned. I try to understand. They feel powerless in return. Their legacy as children of Holocaust survivors compounds the distrust, suspicion, fury. Jews should not be locked up through no fault of their own— especially the weak and the defenseless, the feeble-minded. It's a legacy I can't possibly begin to tackle—especially from such a distance.

I try not to dwell on it. I have friends and family, therapists, social workers, doctors. They support me in my decision. They understand that I feel I have no choice.

Annette is another story.

In the early days of our courtship and marriage, David's work colleague Zach and his girlfriend Annette had been among our closest friends. Zach, from a Greek family in Detroit, and Annette from a large central California Italian Catholic family, were both hilarious: loud, witty, direct, and fun. My style. We attended each other's weddings, shared the stresses and joys of first home purchases, pregnancies, kids' birthdays, hikes, Fourth of July BBQs where Hannah and Joshie played with their boys in their backyard swimming pool. We hired sitters and laughed uproariously through *My Big Fat Greek Wedding*. Zach proclaimed afterward, over tzatziki and dolmas, that the movie wasn't much of an exaggeration. Annette and I agreed that "Greek" in the title could have easily been replaced by "Italian" or "Jewish."

But when I confided to Annette that I was attracted to Mark, she started pulling away. They visited David in the hospital, came to the tiki party.

But to me, especially after David moved to Learning Services, they were cold. I reached out to Annette a few times, to no avail.

I understood. No, I tried to. She was raised in a staunchly Catholic setting where family is paramount. You don't abandon a relative in need. You fulfill your duty. You don't have affairs—at least, if you're a woman.

I want to be angry at her for not understanding, for not supporting me. For ending our friendship.

Instead, I'm just sad. I miss her.

- —.—.— —.

Dr. Winegardner and I meet monthly to evaluate David's situation and discuss issues that arise. David complains of noise and is moved to a quieter room. Despite being cued to use the toilet, he continues to have accidents. He's been mostly compliant, but constantly talks of leaving. One day he's intercepted walking down the long driveway toward the main road, carrying a full backpack. He insists he's going to Lake Tahoe. Another day the police bring him back from the main road walking toward town.

I'm in Dr. Winegardner's office discussing David's "elopement" tendencies. That's their technical term. I wonder what Gabi or Dora would say. Prison break? Dr. Winegardner promises that they'll keep a closer eye on him. I'm not convinced.

"Oh by the way—there's a one-day TBI caregiver conference coming up. Would you be interested in attending? It's at Valley Med—you live close by, don't you?" She rummages on her desk for the brochure.

"But I'm not his caregiver."

She puts down the file and turns to look at me intently. There is real compassion in her green eyes. "Oh, Rachel, of course you are. You're still his wife. You make all of the decisions regarding his care. It doesn't matter that you're not the one changing his diaper or making sure he takes his meds."

I'm not persuaded. "I guess so."

"Let's see." She scans the brochure. "The director of the California Brain Injury Association—they call it CALBIA—is speaking. Also the wife of a TBI survivor. I think you should go. You might learn something. We'll cover the tuition for you."

Though I feel like a fraud, I agree to go.

The morning speakers do tedious power points on legal aspects of TBI, and specific caregiving challenges and strategies. The director promotes a walkathon happening in the fall. I briefly consider attending with the kids, but it's in San Diego. Walkathons have never been my thing. Since her own diagnosis, Mom has tried to get us to attend a yearly walk for pancreatic cancer.

I should do *something*. An idea starts to form—maybe a fundraising concert? I'll talk to the director about it at the break.

I perk up when the afternoon speaker begins her personal account. Two years earlier her husband, wearing a helmet, was sideswiped on his motorcycle. She speaks of raising their teenage children alone, the financial stresses, the challenge of finding caregivers so she can work and get out occasionally. She's living my story, except her husband lives at home since they can't afford to have him in a TBI facility.

Afterward I wait in line to speak to her. Most of the attendees have gone. *Good.* I need to know more about their relationship. I sense that she won't mind my probing.

I tell her a *Reader's Digest* version of my story. "Does your husband make you uncomfortable—um, sexually? Mine occasionally makes comments about my body, which I really don't like. It's weird—he's my husband, but not really." She nods, seems comfortable with my frankness, so I continue. "If you don't mind my asking—do you sleep in the same bed?"

She laughs wryly. "We did at first, but now he's in the guestroom. Which is good because I've been dating. Every few nights he comes in wanting to have sex. I tell him I'm on my period. That works and he goes back to his room."

I stare at her. "Seriously?"

"Yes." She shrugs. "Who knows how long it will work. I'm just happy it does for now."

I head to my car through the familiar hospital corridors. *How does she do it? That could be me. Living a lie.*

No. Impossible.

Thank God I have options.

Chapter 15

MOM LEFT WHEN I WAS SIXTEEN, the summer before my senior year in high school. I was the only kid still at home. She'd fallen in love with a second cousin and moved to New York. She told me she'd been miserable for much of the twenty-seven years married to my father, drowning her despair in vodka. Still the announcement stunned me, baby of the family, the most like her. I adored her. She led my Girl Scout troop, made cookies for bake sales, directed my plays—while my father, though a decent man and a good provider, had affairs and was mostly absent.

The night she left, he cried in my arms. The first time I'd seen him cry.

Dad's tears were harder for me than Mom leaving. At least now the fights would stop. But soon after I realized nothing could be worse. I was desolate without her.

Mom would have made a great hippie, but she was born too soon. She spent the sixties raising kids. I imagine she was envious of the fringe-vested flower children we gazed at from the safety of our car, driving through Golden Gate Park on Sunday outings. She's theatrical, sensitive, generous, pouty, with an acerbic wit. And she suffers from a severe lack of boundaries, a trait she modeled for me. It took me years to learn that it's a good idea—if not imperative—*not* to share each and every feeling immediately. Nor to insist that everyone else does.

Good traits, though, for having people love her. She had a multitude of friends and was always going out for coffee or a meal with someone or another. My high school friends loved hanging out at our house. "How's your mom?" I was repeatedly asked at my twenty-year reunion. "I could tell your mom *anything*. Judy was so cool."

Shortly before my fortieth birthday in 2001, Mom was diagnosed with pancreatic cancer. *That's it*, we all thought. *She'll be gone within a few months.* She'd left me once before. Though only for a few months, I remembered the loneliness, the ache, of feeling motherless.

Hannah and Joshie, four and two, wouldn't remember their grandmother. And in turn, Bar and Bat Mitzvahs, graduations, weddings—she would miss them all.

None of us—Lisa and Paul nor their spouses nor I—could imagine her gone. No Grandma Judy sneaking gummy bears and licorice to the kids (despite strict orders), obsessing over the TV remote when she came to babysit ("How does this thing work? They're so complicated these days!"), beaming in her seat next to me at Hannah's dance recital or Joshie's preschool presentation.

David? He simply refused to accept it. "Judy can't die. It's not going to happen. She's indestructible." And David was right. She endured seven hours of surgery to remove the tumor. And months of radiation and chemo. It seemed that—despite the enormous odds against her—she would be part of the 7% of pancreatic cancer patients to survive. The doctors couldn't believe it. And we breathed a collective sigh of relief.

Yet for the next few years Mom lived beneath the impenetrable cloud of reoccurrence. Digestive issues and fatigue plagued her, made her irritable, petulant. Babysitting the kids became a herculean effort. But she was alive. Alive to dote on her grandchildren, to read to them, to celebrate birthdays and sneak them candy.

A year after David's accident, the cancer recurs. Treatments will prolong her life only slightly. She'll join the other 93%.

We spend the next few months preparing. Inundated with lawsuits, I let Lisa and Paul get Mom's will in order. We take a girls' trip (Lisa, Mom, Susie, and I) to the Napa Valley, laughing as we wipe mud from our eyes at the Calistoga mud baths (agreeing that they're actually slimy and gross). We spend a long weekend in Santa Cruz with Lisa, Gordon, and their kids as Mom grows thin and frail, barely able to walk from our oceanside condo to the beach. Her last escapade.

Mom isn't yet bedridden but will be soon. She chooses hospice over a hospital death.

· — ·— · — — ·

I become fixated on easing the transition for the kids. They've lost their father—as they knew him—so suddenly, so dramatically, so recently. What could I do to prepare them? Especially Hannah, cherished as the only granddaughter—who'd become as attached to Grandma Judy as I had been.

"She's going to miss Hannah's Bat Mitzvah," I moan to my friend Chris over lunch, even though that milestone is three years in the future. Chris runs a hospice organization, knows about grief and death. "At every Bar or Bat Mitzvah that I've performed over the years, I've imagined how it would be for my kids, how happy Mom would be. I pictured her sitting in the front pew, *kvelling*."

"Is there any part of the ritual that can be performed now?" Chris asks. "Maybe Hannah could read a short Torah portion, or do some of the prayers?"

I have a flash. "At our temple the parents give the child a *tallit*, a prayer shawl, in the rabbi's office before the service starts. I could get the *tallit* now, and Mom could present it to her. Hannah will remember Mom whenever she wears it."

Chris looks up from her plate, tears in her eyes.

. —·—·— ·— —··

THE AMAZING MIRACLE BY HANNAH MICHELBERG—CHANUKAH, DECEMBER 3, 2006

I had a memorable experience interviewing my dad, David Michelberg. David was born on June 1st, 1960, to Samuel and Maria Michelberg in Munich, Germany. My dad was 44 when the miracle occurred. On April 19th, 2005, my dad was coming back from a business trip from LA when the plane started to fail. Yaron, the pilot, thought they were over a field and attempted to land the plane. Unfortunately, it was actually a vineyard, not a field. When the plane hit the ground my dad's head hit the windshield. My dad, David, lost sight in one eye, damaged his head from the impact, and broke part of his spine. I think the miracle was that Yaron was still conscious after the accident. If Yaron had not been conscious, they would both be dead. Now they are both alive, living in a hospital. My dad said that these things happen and you just have to go on with your life. He and Yaron are glad they are both still alive, and that they can both still enjoy their families. After the miracle occurred, I know that God will always be there for my family and me. Some people think that if they have a stroke of good luck or something really good

happens, they just say "Oh, it's just my lucky day." But I
think God intervenes because he cares about everything
that lives on the earth.

. — .— — — .

I hear through the grapevine that my college sweetheart and
former fiancé, Brian, is living alone in San Francisco. Still in
the grocery business, never married. Never married? Seriously?
A good looking, 48-year-old, ragingly heterosexual, financially
successful guy? In San Francisco, where straight, single, attractive
women are a dime-a-dozen? *Hmm, is it possible that he's still in*
love with me? Nah. How conceited. He's got to be over me by now.

It happens so fast—overnight—actually. We get together for
a drink and next thing I know he's giving me the PIN number
for his debit card.

I met Brian in a college meteorology class. He loved to
recount (nauseatingly often) that we got together because of his
comment about inversion layers and my remark, "I agree with
you." Brian was slender, had twinkling hazel eyes, impossibly
long girlish lashes, almost-black hair, and a mustache. I've always
been turned on by mustaches.

That moment in meteorology was probably the shining point
in our relationship. After a few exciting months of really fun sex,
I realized we had very little in common and decided to break up
with him. It was the first of our dozen or so breakups—always
initiated by me. Always I got needy and went back to him. To
really make it final (a relative term, I've since discovered), Brian
and I had to get engaged.

Even the engagement was fraught with drama. Brian's company offered him a position in White Plains, New York—an easy
train ride from Manhattan. It was the perfect launchpad for a
struggling singer to make a go of it in the heart of the opera

world. A whirlwind trip East to look at condos, back home to plan the wedding, my worldly possessions (meager though they were) packed on the slow boat to the eastern shore.

That's when I had my first breakdown. Couldn't eat, work, get out of bed. Couldn't breathe. If had known what a panic attack was at the time, I might have done something clinical about it. But at twenty-six, I didn't know where to turn. Sensations of drowning, strangling, suffocating. If I were a believer, I'd have been certain that God was saying, "You idiot. You're about to make the biggest mistake of your life. If I have to cut off your air, turn your stomach inside out, clamp your throat to make you realize it, I will." Miraculously, I listened. I called off the wedding.

Mom's cancer brings us back together—the one silver lining of her horrible illness. That should have been a red flag, or at least a not-so-subtle omen that maybe reuniting wasn't such a great idea. But I'm only seeing what I choose to see, what's convenient, what fits my needs. And God am I needy.

Then Mom has the *chutzpah* to go downhill. Fast. Really dying this time, not just threatening. And Brian falls back into my life. Within the first twenty-four hours, he's given me a full report on his financial status—like a reverse dowry. He starts spending nights at the house, running errands, schlepping kids, paying for meals and outings—taking his turn in the Mom-caretaking rotation schedule that Lisa, Paul, and I have organized so she won't be alone in her condo.

． ．—． ．—． ．．

She is fading, disappearing, cheekbones sharpening, thin legs gone birdlike. She has no appetite. We have to find a way to get her to eat.

Lisa suggests marijuana. Paul and I think it's a great idea— she'll get the munchies, and we'll make sure there's something highly caloric on hand. A milkshake. French fries. Gooey mac and cheese. Anything.

"Absolutely not," Mom declares. "I've worked so hard to stay clean and sober. I'm not going to use any drugs."

We try to reason with her. Pot hasn't been proven addictive. "And anyway, to be honest, you're going to die anyway." That one got a chuckle, but she still resists.

We speak to Mom's doctor, who can't legally recommend it, but he manages to imply that it could definitely increase her appetite. Finally she relents. Brian and I are granted the honor.

I get an overnight sitter for the kids, and we head to Benicia. At Mom's request we pick up Chinese: fried rice, sweet and sour shrimp, beef and broccoli, pot stickers, pork chow mein. The food looks appropriately greasy, thick with calories. I'm hopeful.

Before dinner we pass around a joint that Brian has expertly rolled. Mom coughs despite years of cigarette smoking. We watch her carefully as she picks at her rice.

"I don't feel anything."

"Don't worry, you will," Brian says, catching my amused expression. "Give it a little time."

I've brought a DVD of the movie *Borat*. Neither of them have seen it. We could use a good laugh, and besides, it could be amusing to watch Sacha Baron Cohen pursuing his "Cultural Learnings of America" stoned, with my stoned mother.

"I don't understand," she keeps saying. "Why is he obsessed with Pamela Anderson? Why is he wrestling with that naked fat man? Oh, and is there any more chow mein?"

Brian and I exchange a knowing look. I happily fill another plate with food.

"I'm still not feeling this pot," she complains, shoveling sweet and sour shrimp into her mouth. "It must not be working. Hey— are you going to finish that pot sticker?"

Mom is terrible at keeping secrets. I learn this the hard way. However in this case, it proves to be an advantage.

During one of Brian's shifts, Mom confesses to him how relieved she is that he's come back into my life. "Good timing," she says. She asks him to watch over me and the kids, to protect us, make sure we never need anything. "Please don't tell Rachel I talked to you about this."

The phrase "financial security" is never used, but we all know that's what she means. Talk about an aphrodisiac. Brian's promise to take care of us doesn't make me tremble with desire, but it is seductive. A deal clincher. Neediness + fear + anxiety + desperation + the promise of financial stability = relief. Mom's peace of mind gives her permission to die without guilt. Well, less guilt. And yes, I must admit that a future with security, companionship, and a father for my children drive me back into Brian's willing arms. I ignore the myriad reasons we'd never managed to stay together. I ignore his raging temper tantrums, his constant pot smoking, our lack of anything in common. I ignore the fact that—both intellectually and emotionally—he bores me to death. I ignore the truth: I don't love him.

But Brian is going to take care of us. Mom is happy. As we watch her deteriorate, that's all that matters.

I take Hannah to Alef Bet, our local Judaica shop, to look for a *tallit*. She decides on a pale shade of turquoise and gold in a light gauzy fabric, very soft and feminine (even at ten Hannah has an eye for good design). Since she'll supposedly have it forever, I'm relieved that she doesn't choose a Princess or My Little Pony pattern.

"When is Grandma Judy going to die, Mommy?" Hannah clutches the bag with her precious purchase as we walk to the car.

It's a fair question. I've been very open with both kids about what was going to happen. But I haven't been specific. They don't need details.

I open the car door. "We're not sure. But probably sometime before you get out of school for the summer."

"So she won't come to my birthday party?" Hannah says, buckling her seat belt.

I swallow hard. "No, honey." In the rearview mirror I see her lower lip start to tremble. "That's why we want Grandma Judy to give you the tallit very soon, before she gets too sick." *Before she is pasty, skeletal, wasted on morphine.*

The tears don't come, but I can see Hannah registering the finality of it.

But am I?

That weekend the three of us drive to Mom's. She's now confined to the rented hospital bed in her living room, no longer able to climb the stairs to her bedroom.

Mom places the beautiful *tallit* around Hannah's shoulders, as everyone—even Joshie—recites the prayer for donning the prayer shawl: *Baruch atah adonai, eloheinu melech ha'olam, asher ki'd'shanu b'mitzvotav, vitzivanu, l'hitatef ba tzitzit.*

Mom dies six weeks later, having attended Hannah's Bat Mitzvah after all.

Chapter 16

MOM'S DEATH GRANTS ME A SHORT grace period. Dora—a big fan of Mom's—takes a hiatus from her campaign to get David out of Learning Services. I recognize the kindness. I'm grateful. I want to thank her, but life moves too fast.

The mourning begins.

Paul and Lisa swing into action—schlepping to Goodwill, arranging the estate sale, hiring a real estate agent to sell Mom's condo. Lisa organizes a memorial service at the Unitarian Church she attends. Mom identified as Jewish but didn't have a relationship with a rabbi or temple, so I relent.

"You could sing something, if you want," Lisa offers.

I rarely trust my gut, but this time there's no disconnect between what I thought I should do and what I know I can truly pull off.

"Absolutely not." I'm not sure how I'll act during the service, but the last thing I want to worry about is warming up, rehearsing with an accompanist, and trying to hold back tears. I've never lost someone this close. I suspect it might be a flood.

Should David attend? Paul thinks he might be bewildered by the memorial. Lisa is concerned that he can't sit still for that long, that there might be an outburst.

"David doesn't really have outbursts," I told her. "Yeah, he can be inappropriate but I don't think anything would happen."

David and Mom were close, laughing together over the kids' antics, David teasing Mom about her inability to operate a remote control.

He'll attend.

The church is packed—Mom was so well-loved. The service is beautiful. Cathartic. I sit in the front pew, flanked by the children, David and his caretaker behind us. I cry through Gordon's comments, the pastor's eulogy, the baritone's rendition of *Edelweiss* and *The Impossible Dream*—songs I'd chosen in homage to Mom's love of musical theater. Heaving, wracking sobs. *There is nothing like a mother's love.*

At the reception I'm asked about David, as the questioners glance furtively at him across the room. Where is he living, how long will he stay there, is he improving?

I have rehearsed answers. As we pack leftover cookies and fruit in Tupperware containers, I overhear my friend Dina ask David how he's doing.

"Excellent!" His standard answer. He knows what people want to hear.

If they only knew.

Joshie, Hannah, and I head home. They are quiet, obedient, as if they recognize that our little family keeps shrinking.

- —--- - -

"I'm sorry to hear about Judy," Dora says. "I wish I could have been there for the memorial."

We're having a rare phone conversation. Since the Gabi incident, we communicate only when we have to, usually by email. Dora has hired an American lawyer to help her gain control of David's living situation. I've decided that appointing a neutral conservator would be the right move to avoid any conflict of interest issues with the divorce (I'm still shuddering at that word). There will be a hearing in a few months. Dora plans to contest the conservatorship and suggest herself as the guardian *ad litum*. I'm pissed.

"She was a great lady."

"Thank you."

Silence. My anger gives me permission not to speak. *Whatever.* Why did she call? Surely not just to express her condolences.

She clears her throat. "Um, this is weird, but . . . I've been thinking about David's sexual needs."

In the two years since David's accident, he's never once tried to touch me, unlike the TBI conference speaker's husband. But how could a forty-eight year old man not have desire, despite the mind of a four-year-old? Maslow had named human needs: air, water, sleep, shelter, clothing, sex. Should David be deprived just because I don't want to have sex with him?

"I've thought about it, too."

Dora is thousands of miles away, but I can hear her relief. "I don't even know how to begin to deal with this, and I'm not coming for another month."

"I have some ideas. Don't worry—I'm not going to hire a prostitute. I'll ask around."

I do have ideas. One, anyway. Shortly after breaking it off with Noam, I had dated a guy who was into sadomasochism. I'd been repelled but fascinated, and learned all about the whole S-M underground community. I was adventurous, but not that much. We broke up after a few weeks.

S-M Guy doesn't know how to find a surrogate, but says he'll ask some of his "friends."

Another item to add to the list of things I can do for David and prove to myself I still care.

While waiting for S-M Guy to get back to me, I propose the idea to Nicki, David's case manager.

"We're not supposed to suggest or condone it. Nothing could happen here on campus. And we aren't allowed to drive him to an . . . encounter. But if you drive him there and back, we don't have to know where you're taking him."

I picture picking David up from Learning Services for his outing. "Guess what? We're not going to Best Buy today. Instead, you're going to have sex with a complete stranger!" As I drop him off at a day-use motel, I'd say, "Have fun!" Then I'll wait in the car sipping my Starbucks and browsing Facebook.

Can this get any weirder?

S-M Guy doesn't have any leads, and the idea—noble as it is—takes a back seat for both Dora and me as more pressing matters surface.

We never speak about it again.

Dora's zeal to gain control of David's situation escalates. Over her many visits she's become friendly with some Israelis in San Jose. She enlists the help of my friend Nurit from the kids' school to facilitate a mediation—with me.

Nurit and I discuss it over lunch. "I know two Israeli women," she says. "One is a social worker, the other a therapist. Would you be willing to meet with them together with Dora? She feels much more comfortable speaking in Hebrew." Nurit takes a sip of her iced tea.

I feel cornered by the Israeli army. Not a force I want to oppose.

"I think they'd be impartial," she adds.

It would be good to hash this out. Perhaps Dora will finally see the necessity of maintaining the status quo. But I know

Israelis—especially *sabras*, the native-born. Like the desert cactus: prickly on the outside, soft on the inside. Kindhearted, generous, but direct, loud, aggressive. Can I stand up to them?

What am I—an anti-semite? I shake off feelings of bias against my own people. "Alright. I'll do it."

Nurit smiles. "I'll handle the arrangements." The waitress brings the check. We both reach for it. "I've got this," she says. She gives me a hug as we prepare to leave. "Rachel, it can only bring good to at least talk about it. Wouldn't it be wonderful if you and Dora could come to an understanding?"

"Of course." I'm not hopeful.

I have phone conversations with Devorah and Anat, and trust they'll remain neutral. A few weeks later, the four of us meet on a warm summer evening at the social workers' office.

Dora places a folder on the table. *David Michelberg, Proposal for Life Plan in Israel* on the cover. "We've worked it all out." Her voice is shaky but determined. "It's all in here. In English. He'll live with us and have the basement apartment so he only has to climb one flight of stairs. There are doctors, therapists, psychologists already committed to working with him. He'll have physical therapy three times a week."

She pushes it toward me. Silence. I glance at it. Make no move to pick it up.

"But most importantly," Dora knows how to play her trump card. She pauses, tries to look me in the eye. I remain fixated on my clenched hands on the table. "Most importantly, he'll be with *family*."

Of course, she had to go there. I give myself a silent pep talk: *Stay firm.* "How are you going to pay for it all?" I ask. "David has to stay in the United States until the lawsuit is settled. We've talked about this, Dora." I know my words won't move her, but the two women need to hear my side. "All of the lawyers say it will screw up the case if he leaves. They think David can get a huge award." I'm trying to not sound greedy. "We have to look at the long term."

"Read it." She thumps the folder.

Anat intercedes. "I think it's a good time to separate. Dora, you can go with Devorah, while Rachel and I talk."

Despite Anat and Devorah's best efforts, there's no movement on either side.

Do I think that if Dora hears my position from professionals—in Hebrew—she would understand the stakes? That moving him to Israel now, without enough funding to pay for years of care, could be a disaster? She's not seeing reality. I have to demonstrate being the practical one.

Dora is fighting for her little brother—I admire her tenacity. But so am I.

We are both dug in. Like the mothers and the baby before King Solomon. Right where we started.

I never read the proposal.

- — -— - — -

LETTER FROM JOSHIE
(3RD GRADE SCHOOL ASSIGNMENT) 9/07
Dear Mommy—

My class, Kitah Gimel, *is doing very well. I've been good. I didn't even touch my blue or red name card which is the same as last year. This year no one touched their blue or red name card. I guess we've all been good. I am having a lot of fun with my friends and teacher. My favorite subject is P.E. I like my class.*

From your son,
Joshua

Attorney Mike tells me that Teledyne wants to settle. "We'll see what they're offering," he says. "If it's too low we might be looking at a trial."

"With a jury?" In addition to medical shows, I loved *LA Law, Ally McBeal.* Mom and I had enjoyed watching *Judging Amy* together. Reruns of *Law and Order* helped me get through mandated bed rest toward the end of my pregnancy with Hannah.

"Not sure yet. If we go through a judge, we're dependent on one person's opinion. It would totally depend on who we get. Chances are I'll advise you to go for a jury trial."

I picture myself in the witness box, anxious, sweating. No glamour there.

Mike is correct. After an exhausting all-day meeting in a swanky office at the top of Embarcadero Four with a glorious view of the San Francisco Bay on all sides, Teledyne offers eight million to settle. Mike is holding out for at least fifteen. Of course his firm would get a big chunk, and there would be court expenses and expert witnesses to pay, but that's a lot of money. A *lot.*

Yaron has settled. But his injuries, while extensive, don't prevent him from working for the rest of his life. Nor driving. Nor parenting his kids and being a husband.

Before the jury trial, there's the conservatorship hearing.

I feel like a hamster—running, running, to nowhere. I want it all to be over.

The kids and I meet Bonnie, the proposed conservator, a week or so before the hearing. She is earnest but kind, professional but friendly, and about my age, with two daughters in college. I like her. This could work. I'm ready to give up decision making.

As I make my way to my seat in the hearing room, I'm stunned to see David's closest childhood friend, Jossi, now a high-powered attorney in Munich. *What the fuck is he doing here?*

Lisa has joined me for moral support. "Oh my God, Jossi is here," I whisper.

She squeezes my hand. "You don't have to look at him."

I think about Gabi. "Why does Dora keep showing up with people? I mean, she wants support, but seriously? Jossi? A German attorney? What does she need him for?"

I can't help it. I look at Jossi.

The winter we were in Munich, we went to Jossi's apartment for dinner. We start cooking, since he will be home from work late. Jossi is short and burly, a soccer star in high school, a super athlete. I find him arrogant but fun. He'd asked me to bring as much Rogaine for his receding hairline as I could carry from the States. He thought it was much cheaper than in Europe. I hand him five bottles.

"How much was it?" he asks, pouring himself a beer.

"Expensive. $140."

"What the fuck! That's only a little cheaper than here!"

Hannah began to fuss. I bury my face in her soft hair. What a jerk—he can afford it. I bought the stuff, schlepped it from California along with an infant and all of our baby equipment.

He never thanked me. Pure Jossi.

He glares at me, confirming my suspicions that the whole German contingent hates me. Hated on at least two continents, three if the Middle East qualifies.

I glare back.

The conservatorship is granted to Bonnie. I smile at him.

Chapter 17

BONNIE AGREES THAT DAVID SHOULD STAY at Learning Services for the time being. She visits him regularly—to track his mental progress, moods, therapies, medical condition. She plans to move him into an apartment with a full-time caregiver as soon as the lawsuit is resolved.

With Bonnie overseeing David's care, I've been released from my role as jailor. Aside from crazy Gabi, no one in David's family, not even Dora, ever used that word. I'd cast myself in that position. Now I have a reprieve from playing the villain.

I'm surprised at the sense of liberation. I'm not surprised to notice, though, the undercurrent of doubt about my motivation for producing the fundraising concert for the Brain Injury Association. Is it self-centered to produce an event focused on me and my talent? To garner applause, accolades, attention? Is it driven by guilt? By altruism?

This reflex of berating myself, worrying about what others think, how they judge me—*It has to stop!*

I let it go and am rewarded with a sense of calm, for the moment. I dive into concert prep. As cantor I'd produced concerts and special music services regularly. The professionals with whom I've often worked are motivated: the soprano, baritone, tenor, pianist. They are all close friends. The JCC where my kids attend school offers their spacious social hall, gratis. A local celebrity TV reporter agrees to emcee. A former congregant will organize and bake for the reception.

California Brain Injury Association officials fly up from San Diego to attend. We sing duets, trios, the quartet from *Rigoletto*. The event is a great success, raising nearly $4,000. David is there smiling, bewildered. He sits between Hannah and Joshie in the front row. For one night, I feel proactive, caring.

I'm doing what I can.

- — - — - — -

"Joshie!" I shriek. "Come back here right now and put on your helmet!"

He's riding his scooter down the driveway. "Mommy, it's not a big deal. People don't fall very much on scooters. I'll be careful."

Disbelief. I shake my head. How many times have I told them? My kids, of all people, will always wear a helmet.

In 2010, it is yet to be discovered that traumatic brain injury is pervasive in the NFL. But American soldiers encountering IEDs in Afghanistan and Iraq have been returning with brain injuries. I hear interviews with their spouses—mostly women—on NPR. They have committed to caring for their permanently changed, debilitated husbands.

They have no idea.

I wish them strength.

- — - — - — -

I keep searching for activities to engage us as a family. Learning Services is near Hecker Pass, a lovely stretch of wooded winding road. A county park is at the top of the pass. I assume there's an easy trail or two in this farm country dotted with wineries, nurseries, and fruit stands. It's October, the leaves are turning. We might be able to pick up a few pumpkins en route.

Hannah is at a birthday party, so Joshie and I pick David up. "Has he been to the bathroom recently?" I ask Lupe, my favorite of David's caregivers. Part of his protocol requires cueing him to use the toilet every two hours.

Incontinence is common with TBI survivors. It's usually not physiological, rather a disruption between the body signaling and the brain taking action. With damaged brain circuitry, the messages may be sent—but not received.

"Yes, but I'm not sure if he did anything in there. Maybe we should try again?"

"It's OK." I glance at Joshie. He is staring at Angie, the blind woman, standing in the kitchen doorway as usual, rocking from side to side. She seems a little sharper than the other residents— always greeting us and interested in what we're doing or where we're going. I don't feel like having another "teaching" moment. I'm eager to leave.

"He's ready to go, right?" I glance at Joshie again. He doesn't know his father wears diapers. I've spared David some humiliations. Lupe assures me he's ready.

The drive is picturesque—soothing even—and I'm in a good mood. A welcome change. The park seems eerily empty for a beautiful Sunday in October. I appreciate the serenity as much as the natural beauty.

At the trailhead is an emergency call box.

Shit. What was I thinking? I'm about to go hiking in the wilderness with a seven-year-old and a brain-injured grown man. David could have a seizure or a stroke. Any one of us could trip and break a leg or an ankle. I check my phone. Confirmed: no cell signal.

Maybe we should turn back. I thought this would be a whole-some, healthy family activity. But then what would we do? Damn, can't I ever win? I'm such an idiot.

"Here we are. Everybody out!" I chirp. Sometimes my acting skills come in handy. *We're here now. Deal with it.*

Completely oblivious to my fears, Joshie scrambles out of the car and runs down the trail while I help David out of his seatbelt. "Whoa, bud!" I call. "Daddy can't go that fast. Wait for us!"

We work our way down the trail slowly. It's steeper than I anticipated. David's gait is labored. Not unusual. The woods are serene, eucalyptus-scented. The only sound is the crunching of the leaves under our feet, and Joshie's occasional cries of, "Mommy, hurry up!" Gradually, I relax.

The first half mile is pure descent. I'm deciding we shouldn't go very far when David stops abruptly. He refuses to walk—grimacing and grunting.

"David, you OK?" He doesn't answer but walks in the wrong direction. Slowly. The odor is unmistakable.

"Eww, what's that smell?" Joshie's high-pitched voice. "Yuck!"

I wave dismissively. "Oh it must be some animal poop." How can I prevent Joshie from coming to understand? I desperately try to preserve some semblance of parental respect and reverence for David.

"Why don't you run on ahead? Daddy and I will catch up." If I keep them far enough apart—and David downwind—perhaps Joshie won't figure it out. Thank God David is wearing a diaper.

It seems to take hours to reach the car. David walks gingerly, though he says nothing about what must be very uncomfortable. Maybe he's oblivious. A mixed blessing.

As we pull out of the parking area we pass the call box. I'd worried about an emergency. This isn't—no broken bones nor blood nor seizures. But it feels worse. A reminder that David is—in many ways—like a toddler. Except toddlers can be potty trained. For David nothing is certain.

I open all the windows and make sure Joshie isn't sitting behind David. "A whole new world . . ." I sing loudly with Jasmine and Aladdin. Distraction usually works well.

"We're back!" I call to Lupe. She comes out of the kitchen. "David needs to go to the bathroom."

She instantly knows what happened. "Don't worry, we'll take care of it." She puts her hand on the small of David's back. "David, would you like to take a shower now?"

I see the hint of a halo over Lupe's head. I mentally promise to recommend her for sainthood. She has officially joined Lois and Christina's club.

David dutifully follows without looking back.

"Bye Daddy!" Joshie calls down the hall after David. He scowls. "Daddy didn't say bye."

"I guess he really had to go. We'll see him next week. C'mon, bud, let's go home."

I realize we never did get those pumpkins.

Chapter 18

NOTE FROM JOSHIE (SLIPPED UNDER MY DOOR)
I know I have been the worst kid, but I am EXTREMELY
mad. But I am in my room, thinking of what I've done.
And I know you've worked hard, I know that I'm very
selfish, teasing, inaproapreat (don't know how to spell it)
dumb, lazy kid who doesn't deserve to be forgived. So I
will ground myself for the whole week!!
From your son,
Joshua

I can't remember a time before single parenthood—when I had
a partner to share decision making, disciplining, driving to dance
class, theater rehearsal, baseball practice. Helping with home-
work. Refereeing constant fights. Fulfilling required volunteer
hours. Stopping at the grocery store for a forgotten item. I'm
jealous of divorced friends whose custody agreements provide
occasional weekends off.

I go to Joshie's third grade teacher conference. Alone. The teacher is kind but direct. Joshie has an amazing ability to decode, she says. A nearly photographic memory. Excellent in math and spelling. He is sweet, super inquisitive. In fact, she has had to put a limit on how many questions he asks so that he doesn't monopolize class time. But though he can read any book almost flawlessly, he isn't comprehending what he's reading. It's beginning to be a problem, since they are moving into chapter books, with fewer pictures. Moving forward he will need reading intervention or he'll fall behind.

Joshie is also having social issues. He continually seeks out adult approval, but does not pick up innuendo or social cues from the other children. He's often inflexible, easily frustrated, and pouts if he feels he's failed at something. His classmates become impatient with his humor or attempts to be "cool."

We discuss strategies. Possible reading tutors. I look into it: $120/hour. *Ka-ching ka-ching. I'm struggling to make ends meet already, I'm supposed to be handling this out of the support I'm getting. Can I ask Bonnie to help?*

I leave, drained and despairing. Overwhelmed with the burden. How do I help my child? Ensure that he will have the tools he needs to succeed, to thrive? Coach him on making friends—and keeping them? As I descend the staircase, a moan escapes and I have to hold the handrail. My legs crumple, and I'm sitting on the steps, weeping. The weight of responsibility for my little human—my flesh and blood—is crushing. *How can I help my son? David, I need you. I can't do this alone.*

As I crouch sobbing, I feel someone's eyes on me. It is the father of Hannah's classmate. I sniffle and wipe my nose on the back of my hand. I am embarrassed. "Sometimes it's just too much, you know?"

He doesn't try to comfort me, or offer words of wisdom. Just stands there, staring.

It's hard to escape the onslaught of child development information. From *What to Expect When You're Expecting* to Las Madres to breastfeeding support groups, young mothers are deluged with timelines, charts, expectations. I never dreamed that I would be one of those paranoid mothers who run to the pediatrician with every scratch, fever, developmental delay or quirky behavior. But there I was, drowning in projections: Oh no, she's four months old and not rolling over yet? What's wrong with him, he's supposed to be crawling already. Shouldn't she be sleeping through the night by now?

I considered myself to be doing a reasonable job parenting my small children, yet every deviation from the norm brought questions and inevitable doubts: *Maybe I'm doing something wrong. Maybe David is doing something wrong. Maybe I shouldn't have taken those antacids in the third month or had that glass of wine in the seventh.*

Despite the standard anxiety, we were pretty sure both kids were fine. Children don't read the child development books. They'll hit milestones when they're good and ready.

But unlike Hannah, who'd spoken early and often, Joshie still wasn't putting more than two words together at age three. David insisted that we have him tested.

"Boys are different, " I protested. "For God's sake, he can recite the alphabet already. You know how he recognizes letters everywhere and points them out. He's probably extremely gifted, just has different skills. You're being paranoid."

David wasn't deterred, so I reluctantly arranged for testing through our local school district. During the session—which I was sure was a waste of time—the professionally dressed, well-meaning psychologist narrowed her eyes as she watched golden-haired, chubby-cheeked Joshie on the floor. He was repeatedly spinning a plastic bowl on its rim, clapping with glee as it twirled, delighting in the click it made as it came to rest.

"Does he often engage in repetitive behaviors?" the doctor inquired.

I felt my jaw tensing with defense of my child, my curly blonde boy. "Not really," I mumbled. "He's just playing with the bowl," I said louder. "All kids do that. My daughter did that."

I was lying. Hannah never played with bowls that way.

The doctor looked at me, pity plain on her face. "Yes, some of them do," she demurred. I didn't fail to notice that she started jotting something in her notebook—something entirely false and overly analytical, I was certain.

The test results came back a month later. Joshua Michelberg, age three years four months, may be on the autism spectrum, which qualified him for special services from the district. Re-test prior to kindergarten entry.

Nothing conclusive, I told David, resisting the inevitable I-told-you-so.

That summer, Joshie's speech improved. "More juice. Big doggy. Don't want. Bad Hannah." He began to make the connection that his beloved alphabet letters actually had a purpose, that they could be put together to make sounds. He started easily reading simple words in picture books that Hannah, nineteen months older, was still sounding out. Joshie was also fascinated with maps, able to identify states by their shape and location. "Mi-ni-sooo-tah!" he'd shriek happily. "A-lah-skah! Verr-mont"! David and I were delighted, not to mention relieved. In a few short months our beautiful baby had gone from the certainty of a life filled with struggle to that of a *wunderkind*, a genius, a child prodigy—Mozart, a Picasso.

The following winter, his preschool director voiced her concerns at our parent-teacher conference.

I reached for David's hand. This wasn't good. "I know this is hard to hear, but I think Joshie might be on the autism spectrum." She leaned forward, pursing her lips sympathetically. "I really think you should have him evaluated."

Now it was David's turn. I could practically hear him sneering. I pulled my hand away.

We drove home mostly in silence. "It has to be a psychiatrist this time," he insisted as we turned onto our street.

"Why?" *My baby, going to a shrink?* "Psychiatrists only prescribe meds. Joshie isn't depressed. A psychologist would be perfectly fine."

David turned off the car and yanked the keys out of the ignition. "No. Find a psychiatrist. If you don't, I will."

Why is it always my job? Joshie is his kid, too. I opened my mouth to continue the argument but closed it again. *What the hell,* I thought. *I still can't admit it but maybe David's right. Pick your battles.*

Off we went, Joshie and I. The doctor seemed experienced and had a melodic Italian name. The waiting room was drab and didn't have a lot of toys. What's the kid supposed to do while we're waiting, read *Scientific American?*

Finally we were called in. The doctor's office was also dull but at least there were a few toys—puzzles, blocks, Legos, a Slinky. The doctor motioned me to take a seat. Joshie immediately found the slinky. "So what's going on?"

Not new to therapy, I was prepared. "Joshie's preschool director said I should have him tested." As I told his story, Joshie sprawled on the floor pulling the slinky open and watching as it snapped back into shape, again and again. *Please,* I prayed silently. *Don't. Stop. Please, pass the test. Play with something else. Do the puzzle, build a Lego house. My sweet boy. You don't know what's at stake here.*

But Joshie didn't stop. He kept snapping the slinky open and closed, again, and again, and again.

As my story wound down, I was asked to leave. Reluctantly I retreated to the dreary waiting room while my progeny's future was being decided. After the longest thirty minutes of my life I was called back into the doctor's ugly office.

"There is no question," the doctor said, right in front of my son. "Joshie has Asperger's syndrome. On a scale of one to ten, he is a seven or eight."

"Ten being the best?" I stammered, already knowing the answer to the question.

The doctor shook his head.

I gazed at the pink-cheeked towheaded child stacking blocks at my feet. He was exactly the same boy he'd been that morning when I helped him brush his teeth, tied his shoes.

But he was no longer a *wunderkind*—he was challenged. "Special." On the spectrum.

·—·—·—··

Enough of stories. Time to change the things I can. It's been clear to everyone else for two years. It's a conversation I've been avoiding for months. It's time. I need to tell David he won't be coming home. I've hashed out the scenario in therapy for months, role-playing with Nancy and Sue. With David, however, it isn't a true dialogue. How much he will understand? Will he just pretend to understand?

Dr. Winegardner suggests that she and Dr. Poncé, David's psychologist at Learning Services, be present. I'm grateful for the support, for the buffer. She advises that we focus on the living situation. We won't mention the divorce. Not yet. One major blow at a time.

How do you tell someone they're being rejected—evicted from their own home—through no fault of their own? This must be what it's like to be the boss who has to lay people off. Worse—I promised to love and honor. Obviously I can't control what my heart does, but honoring is more complex. Vowing to honor our children is not verbalized in public.

We meet at Learning Services in a small dining room that smells faintly of fried food. David is compliant, docile. He has no idea what's coming.

We settle into chairs, David between the two doctors. I clear my throat. "I guess I should start."

Dr. Winegardner gives me a tight smile that says: go on, get it over with.

I fiddle with my purse straps. Everyone's waiting for me to start. *This is like that audition when I blanked. No idea which words are supposed to come next, despite hours of practice.* I force myself to look up. "David, we need to talk about the future. About where you're going to be living."

He sits up a little straighter. "I live in Willow Glen," he says confidently.

I chew on the inside of my cheek. My heart is pounding.

"That's what we're here to discuss." Dr. Poncé looks pointedly at me, waiting.

The words stick in my throat. *I'm bombing this audition. I'm definitely not getting this part.*

Dr. Winegardner raises her eyebrows toward me. I give a little nod. "We want you to know that you will always be cared for, David," she says. "Rachel is feeling very sad about this, but she isn't able to take you home to San Jose."

"I go to San Jose a lot," David says. "The short Mexican guy takes me in the van."

I find my voice. "David, we mean that you're going to stay here at Learning Services for a little while longer. Then maybe you'll move to your own apartment, or even go to live with Dora, in Israel."

"I live on Meredith Avenue. Joe lives next door. There's a Noah's Bagels down the street." David's blue eyes—even the blind one—are clouded with uncertainty.

"I'm really sorry, David, it's too hard for me. I can't take care of you at home." I shift on my chair. "With the kids and all." *Don't explain too much, Dr. Winegardner had warned. Keep it simple.* "You can visit, but you won't live on Meredith any more."

David's eyes narrow. The crevasses in his forehead deepen. "You bitch."

There's no reasoning, no arguing, no cajoling. I didn't think he'd have the capacity to challenge me. I'm glad for the reprieve. "I'm so, so sorry." *I sound stupid.*

Dr. Poncé responds to David's agitation. "Rachel, maybe you and Dr. Winegardner should wait in her office while I talk to David."

I'm relieved. Ridden with guilt, but relieved. That's all? Shouldn't I have to suffer more? Be forced to feel the full wrath of David's rage?

David has gotten up and is slowly pacing around the room. I'm frozen to my chair.

"Yes, Rachel, let's go." Dr. Winegardner gives me a look and I follow her toward the door. I turn to say again: *I'm sorry.*

But David's back is to me. I say nothing.

He can't care less that I'm sorry.

Chapter 19

JUST KEEP SWIMMING. DORY'S ADVICE TO NEMO—and herself—is wise. Her advice becomes my mantra. I find a reading specialist for Joshie and pick him up from school early every Monday and Wednesday for tutoring. Putting my tail firmly between my legs, I reach out to Bonnie for assistance with the $120 session fee. She agrees to pay half in addition to the support I'm already getting.

Beverly, the tutor, explains: When a neurotypical (the current PC phrase) person reads, they create pictures—movies almost—to visualize the story. This capacity is often missing in kids on the autism spectrum. This explains why Joshie's comprehension is so much better with picture books—he can "see" the story in his mind. Words alone don't cut it.

But he can't read from picture books his whole life.

In addition to the work she's doing with Joshie, Beverly recommends that instead of me reading to him at bedtime, he read aloud to me and then summarize in his own words. I can help by offering specific, direct questions: "How did Fern take care of her newborn pig Wilbur? Why would Willy Wonka be concerned about spies in his factory?" Paragraph by paragraph. It is a painful, laborious process. Joshie gets impatient and just wants to read to get to the end of the chapter. He doesn't care whether he understands. Hannah, eavesdropping instead of reading her own book, is incredulous that her brother isn't getting it. I hide my own incredulity. I tell her to read in her own room.

Just keep swimming.

Mike and Kristine and their staff are gearing up for the trial, which has been set for September, 2008. First though, the defense has requested a deposition, hoping to discredit my loss of consortium claim—they've learned that my marriage was already on shaky ground when the accident happened.

Mike preps me. "Don't offer any information. Your answers should be limited to "yes," "no," and "I don't remember" whenever possible. Sometimes you'll have to say more, but keep it short. They're also going to ask questions that will delve into your marital problems and other relationships with men, to establish that maybe you didn't really lose all that much."

"Great." *Worse than I expected.*

Mike notices my dread. "Their attorneys' job is to minimize your loss from his accident. Don't be surprised if they bring up the kids' problems, too."

The deposition takes place in downtown Willow Glen, just a few blocks from our house. There are several defense attorneys present. One of the Teledyne lawyers, who has flown up from LA, is young and earnest. "He looks inexperienced," Mike whispers to me. "This could be good for us."

We shake hands. The videographer and stenographer signal that they're ready to start. I'm nervous but remind myself to take deep breaths. That helps. I fiddle with my wedding ring—I've put it back on for the occasion. (Is that a not-so-subtle deception? Maybe.) I remind myself that I'm on my turf, my neighborhood—my yoga studio is just a few doors down. I try to channel that sense of calm. That fails.

Everyone identifies themselves for the record. Young earnest guy starts. "Alright. Mrs. Michelberg, who is Mark Berman?

Jesus. Right off the bat?

I look him right in the eye. "A musician."

Mike stifles a laugh, and the earnest attorney shifts in his seat. He asks if I had a relationship with Mark before the accident. Then asks about Brian—if I intend to marry him, how much time he spends at our house. I'm evasive about marriage intentions but admit that Brian spends more time at our house than at his San Francisco condo.

The questioning shifts to probing into our family's mental health history. How long I have taken anti-depressants and why. How long and how often I have been in therapy and why. He starts in on the kids.

Q. How often has Hannah seen her therapist?

A. It has varied. But the average would be once every two weeks. At first it was once a week. We thought that Hannah was doing a little bit better in the beginning of this school year. So around the fall of 2007. But then she started having troubles again, so we went back.

Q. What type of troubles?

A. (starting to tear up) I need a minute.

Q. Sure. I understand.

A. Hannah suffers from anxiety. She, I believe, suffers from some depression, although that manifests itself differently depending on the time and what's going on in her life. She has recently been diagnosed with ADHD and PTSD. She has a great deal of trouble sleeping. She is very afraid of being away from me, and this has gotten better with therapy. She's grown a little and felt more comfortable with herself and her safety with me. But she—she acted like a two-year-old as far as separation anxiety for the first year and a half after the accident where—if I left the house—she would call me every five minutes and want to know exactly where I was and when I was coming home, and she would cry and carry on. She was in a lot of pain, and it comes and goes. And it's often related to how happy she is at school or with her friends. Right now she's going through a very difficult period again. Does that answer your question?

Q. Yes, thank you. And I apologize for having to take you through that, but for a number of reasons I need to ask certain questions. If there was any way around it, believe me, Mrs. Michelberg, I would try to do that.
A. Thank you.

He continues, trying to establish that all of us had issues before the accident. I try not to show my disdain. How could anyone think that this tragedy was just a blip on our screens? That we were fucked up before, so the accident can't be to blame?

Q. Alright. Has anyone ever told you that they think—or it's their opinion—that those diagnoses are a direct result of Mr. Michelberg's accident?
A. I can't conclusively say that. The psychiatrist said that that was the likely cause. I believe our situation is somewhat unique, but I'm not sure.

Q. Pardon me if I ask, but what do you mean by unique?

A. That the combination of a tragic accident like this without the benefit of closure has—is an unusual situation. That children—many children with ADHD, or even adults, have not necessarily had to deal with the kind of loss at seven or eight years old. And I—I feel very isolated.

Q. I appreciate the answer. You mentioned the word "closure." What do you mean?

A. There's been a kind of a death in our family. It's a death of David, their father and my husband, as I knew him, as they knew him. They see him, and he isn't the same person. He isn't a father. He isn't able to be a husband in the way that he was. So there is very little closure for us.

Q. Would resolution of this lawsuit bring closure to you?

A. Resolution of this lawsuit would greatly assist in bringing closure.

Q. How would that help?

A. I wouldn't have to relive all of this. It's—it feels like—it feels like the night of the accident all over again. Every time I see the look in my daughter's eyes when she doesn't know what to say to her father—I see that she wants to talk to him. She wants to relate to him, but she has no idea how. It's very painful. Every visit is painful. As a parent, when your children are in pain, it's much worse.

When I go to an event that they're proud of and I bring David to it and he sees their play or their performance or their milestone ceremony at their school, and he sits there and smiles. But he—they know that he doesn't—he doesn't understand what they really accomplished. I'm sorry. What was the question?

Hour after agonizing hour, I'm being grilled about our family, my relationships, my financial situation, who I confide in, what we discuss; every therapist or mental health professional I've consulted. I'm exhausted and we haven't discussed Joshie yet.

Q. Let's talk about Joshua. What was it about Joshua's behavior or anything else that you consider that he needed to see a mental health professional in the spring of 2007?

A. He'd been expressing some envy of Hannah, who was seeing a person who we described as someone she could talk to and express her feelings to. At the same time I noticed Joshua's behavior was difficult to manage. He had a hard time listening, following instructions, staying still. The most—I would say the most overwhelming aspect of his behavior that pushed me in that direction was his desperate need for attention. He would do anything to get it. Constant stream of words, movement, Mommy look, Mommy look, Mommy Mommy Mommy—and whoever else was around, but mostly me. And I felt that maybe he was acting out, an emerging awareness of his lack of a parent, to try and compete for my attention. I felt that some therapy at that time would be very helpful for him, as it had been for Hannah.

They were especially interested that I had admitted wanting a divorce.

Q. Do you intend to file for divorce?
A. Yes.

Q. Have you ever discussed the fact with Brian that you would like to get this lawsuit resolved before you get married to him?
A. Yes.

Q. Is there a reason for that?
A. I think it makes sense.

Q. Why does it make sense?
A. Because there needs to be closure somewhere. Right now I'm in a state of limbo with status, with ability to make decisions about the future. Being able to move ahead with my life and my children's lives. Knowing what kinds of financial decisions we can make—if I can send them to a private school or do they need to attend public school? My daughter is going to need braces. And questions about where David is going to be. The state of his health. So the more closure we can get and the more avenues we can get, the better. He has a permanent disabling brain injury that will prevent him from working in any kind of meaningful way. It will preclude him from being independent. He's lost everything.

And I—I'm trying to do the right thing, but it's—it's not always clear what that is. What's right for one person isn't right for another. And there's a lot of judgment and a lot of emotion that comes into something like this.

So I just think—I know this is a general answer to your question but I think the more that is settled, the more we understand exactly what the stakes are, exactly what the legal status is, the better.

Q. You want to get this lawsuit resolved before you file for divorce?
A. Well, at least.

Q. What else?

A. I want my children to be ready for that. They are still very young, but they're really in this phase of understanding more and more. They're not teenagers where I can sit down and tell them exactly what is going on and this is what you can expect.

But I have been doing a little more of that with them, particularly my older one. Sometimes it comes out of their questions, and sometimes it comes out of me feeling like they're ready to know.

But there is—there is nothing more important to me than my children. And I think David would have wanted them to be placed first, no matter what.

They've had too much loss. So that's my answer.

It's a marathon. Questions about Mark, the restraining order I took out on Diane, the conservatorship, whether or not I approved of Bonnie's decisions for David's care. My relationship with Dora. Gabi. The bank fiasco. All of it. They seem to know my whole life story and the names of everyone I'd ever talked to about David.

That's just Day One.

The first hour of Day Two focuses on my therapy. Is it true I've seen Nancy since I was nineteen? What have we discussed, before and after the accident? How long have I been depressed? Medications I take for back pain, sleep. Then:

Q. What are your children's reactions to David's visits?

A. It's very hard. They don't interact with him as much as I would like them to. I try to encourage it. They are kind to him. I have to tell them to go sit next to Daddy, hold his hand. Sit on his lap, or show Daddy your picture you drew or show him your report card. Sit with Daddy and watch a movie. They tend to gravitate toward me, so it's very awkward.

But I think it's—I've done the best that I can. I don't know what more I can do besides try to find things that they can do together. Play a computer game—sometimes that works. So I would say it's a strained atmosphere, but there is no animosity. There is no anger.

Q. Has he ever said or done anything untoward towards your children or to you when he visits?
A. No. He's made a couple of comments to me that would be natural in a normal marriage relationship. For example, about his desires. It makes me uncomfortable but I understand them. So I just change the subject.

Q. Does he say these things in front of the children?
A. No.

Q. Have you ever discussed with your children whether they're uncomfortable when David visits . . .
A. Yes.

Q. . . . or whether they find it to be a burden?
A. I haven't used those words. I've told them that we're going and there's no choice. That we're going to go. I try to make it fun for them so that it's not just a burden and something they will learn to dread.

Q. What do they say to you before or after he visits about him coming over?
A. Sometimes they're extra whiny after a visit. More so when

they were younger, the first few years after David's accident. It's—they just manifest their bad behavior with me.

I try to foster their relationship with him so that he's a part of their lives, even if it's just a small part. He comes to their plays. He comes to their dance performances. He's there for important school events. That's the way I've tried to structure it so that they'll identify him as their father and not just some—you know—weird guy in a place with lots of weird people.

Q. And now that he comes and visits you on Sundays rather than you travelling to Gilroy, have the children's reactions changed at all?
A. Not much. They feel more comfortable in their home. They feel more comfortable not needing to be around other residents who are having outbursts or strange behavior. That happens very often down there.

Q. When David comes to visit, does he seem to have a positive reaction?
A. He smiles a lot and tries to make conversation. He seems to enjoy watching the kids do whatever they're doing. I ask him sometimes to help me make dinner, and he sometimes grumbles about that, but he chops a vegetable or whatever it is I ask him to do. He's very placid.

Every lawyer gets their turn, with Mike interjecting often that I've already been asked this or that question. They ask about Noam and a guy named Scott whom I had dated a few times, and again about Brian and Mark. I'm being methodically stripped, layer by layer, of any shred of dignity I've worked so hard to attain.

Though I'd been sitting for two days, Mike drives me home, two blocks away. I don't have the energy to walk.

"You did well," he says, as I sit in his car looking at our house.

I can't find the strength to move my legs, to open the car door. My body feels drained but heavy. How can I face the kids now? This flawed, exposed, shell of a mother. I'm torn between allowing the shame to show and pasting on the accustomed smile.

"Don't worry," Mike says as I drag myself out of the car. "They don't have much. I think you'll be sympathetic to the jury."

It's only March. I have to wait another six months to find out.

·—·—·—··

The summer limps along. I have a job as cantor for a synagogue in San Mateo for the High Holy Days—the distraction of preparing and rehearsals with the choir helps alleviate my anxiety over the impending trial. Since the '70s, synagogue music has been moving away from the classical style, toward a more campy, folksy, Kum-ba-ya approach, but for the Holy Days we keep it more traditional and I'm happy letting my operatically trained voice loose.

Brian and I are still talking about marriage. Daily, I shake off the discomfort of déjà vu—the familiar memories that he isn't right for me. *We don't have enough in common; he smokes too much pot; he has a terrible temper; he bores me. But the kids like him; he worships me; he's a good guy. I'll deal with it after the trial.*

"After the trial." My new mantra.

Mike and Kristine are going full throttle. Their whole office seems to be involved in preparation, not much for me to do but wait. I'll be a minor player, though the outcome will determine the future for all of us. Will I have to sell the house? Will there be any money at all for the kids' college? Will we have to leave San Jose for a less expensive area where I'll have to start from scratch with my voice studio? New schools, new friends, new community. Just keep swimming.

And for David. There's money from the workers' compensation settlement, but he could live a long time. Is it enough to take care of him?

Jury selection starts in late August, shortly after the kids start school. Mike tells me that it's an arduous process and I don't have to be there the whole time, but my intention is to attend the proceedings as often as possible. I completely miss the fact that both Rosh Hashanah and Yom Kippur conflict with the trial.

"It's OK," Mike says. "Just come when you can."

Somehow I manage to get myself to the synagogue and sing the services without fainting from anxiety over the trial. Thank God for twenty years of performing.

Almost every morning after dropping the kids at school I schlep myself to the courthouse, where a parade of specialists on both sides—economists, mechanics, psychiatrists—drone on about aviation engineering and maintenance, the potential cost of caring for a fully disabled man, how long David might live. Charts and graphs. The jurors—nine women and three men—look as bored as I feel.

I'm astonished when the defense attorney asserts—through illustrations and simulations—that Yaron, the pilot, bears some of the responsibility for the crash. That he could have made his emergency landing on a different field.

Seriously? I catch Kristine's eye, and she shrugs. *This is how it works—they're doing their job.* I don't love flying. I disliked small planes even before the crash—before the terrifying flight long ago through the fog in Monterey. But I wonder what that attorney would have done in the same situation. In my book, Yaron is a hero. The two men survived a fucking plane crash. Who does that?

Friends and family come to sit with me. Lisa, Gordon, Sue, Julie, Dina. My attorney friend Nora sits with me for two days, whispering translations of legalese in my ear. Jessica makes the two-hour drive from Folsom. It's good to have folks to go to lunch with, to decompress, to help interpret the complexities of the expert testimony. One day Learning Services brings David for a few hours. Mike wants the jury to see him. Bonnie, who has been there most days (prompting me to wonder how many billable hours she is logging), sits next to David. I'm a few rows behind. I feel slightly jealous that she's the one with a hand on his knee, with the reassuring looks.

Careful what you ask for.

A few weeks into the trial I turn on NPR as usual on my drive home. "Lehman Brothers, a giant player in the investment banking industry, collapsed today amid financial meltdown. Reports that Bear Stearns is also about to dissolve are also surfacing. It is possible that the United States is about to enter a recession that could rival the Great Depression of 1929."

Is the whole world falling apart? I drive the few miles home, for the millionth time wondering what the hell is going to happen to us. *Please, God, let my assets, my house be secure. Let me have the resources to send my children to college. Don't let the world dissolve just as my little world is starting to come together, to move toward normalcy.*

・—・—・—・—・・

Mike preps me to testify. He will ask questions about our marriage, David's commitment to the kids. He needs to establish how much I've lost. As if anyone could know.

I'm on the stand for maybe ten minutes. The defense doesn't even question me. One of the jurors—a woman about my age—smiles at me, compassion in her eyes. A welcome anti-climax.

The trial wraps up after five weeks with less-than-dramatic closing arguments from both sides. "How long before the verdict?" I ask.

"No way of knowing," says Mike. "I'll call you when the jury returns."

He calls on Day Five. "Sometime this afternoon."

Brian gives me a kiss as I head out the door. "I know you're nervous. It will be OK." I rally a weak smile.

In the corridors outside the courtroom we wait. And wait. Gordon is there, and Lisa. Mike paces for hours, doing laps around the floor of the courthouse. I join him intermittently. Walking helps.

The owner of Aviation Classics—the "popsicle stand" maintenance facility in Reno who serviced the plane—approaches me. "Can I talk to you for a minute?"

I pat the seat on the bench next to me. "Sure."

"Thanks, I'll stand." He looks miserable. "We haven't really ever talked . . . I know how much you've lost. I just wanted to say how terribly sorry I am for any role my business had in this accident."

So I'm not the only one with guilt.

I want to give him a hug, but it seems awkward. I look up at him, hoping to convey forgiveness. I've never blamed him or his mechanics. "Thank you so much for saying that. I really appreciate it."

We exchange sad, grateful smiles. I watch him walk away. *So many have been damaged. If Aviation Classics is found negligent, he will lose his business. But most of us can rebuild. David can't.*

I cry quietly. And wait.

Late that afternoon, as we resign ourselves to having to return the following day, there is a flurry of activity. "The jury's returned," Mike says through slightly gritted teeth. "Let's go in."

My heart is pounding harder than it ever had on any opening night. Lisa grips my hand.

The forewoman hands the judge the verdict.

Q. Was Aviation Classics negligent?
A. Yes.

Q. Was Aviation Classics' negligence a substantial factor in causing the engine failure?
A. Yes.

Q. Was Teledyne Continental Motors negligent?
A. Yes.

Q. Was Teledyne Continental Motors' negligence a substantial factor in causing the engine failure?
A. Yes.

Q. Was Yaron Ekshtein negligent?
A. Yes.

Apportionment of fault is outlined. Teledyne—35%. Aviation Classics—55%. Yaron Ekshtein—10%. I am glad that Yaron isn't here and wonder about the repercussions for him. *Hasn't he suffered enough?*

Damages for David are pronounced, one at a time. I'm confused with the amounts, trying to keep track—I look at Mike and Kristine who are attempting to keep their faces neutral but failing.

"So . . . we won?" I whisper to Kristine.

She nods with a glance at Mike. "We did very well."

David is awarded over thirteen million dollars: past and future economic loss of earning capacity and medical expenses; past and future non-economic loss including physical pain, mental suffering, depression, loss of enjoyment of life, loss of freedom, loss of ability to parent, loss of dignity, loss of independence, disfigurement, physical impairment, grief, anxiety, humiliation, emotional distress.

David will be set for the rest of his life. Thank God. It's a consolation. But at such a price.

The jury accepts my loss of consortium claim. I'm awarded $250,000. The attorneys will take their share of $40,000, but we can stay in our house—at least for the time being. We'll be OK. I exhale.

As we leave the courtroom, I catch the eye of the juror who had gazed at me sympathetically during the trial.

Hang in there, say her eyes.

Thank you, say mine.

Chapter 20

BONNIE SERVES ME WITH DIVORCE PAPERS a week later. I'm a little stunned. Resentful—that was supposed to be *my* privilege, *my* right. I'll comply but am annoyed that she moved so quickly, usurped my upper hand.

The kids and I are rehearsing *Oliver!* together that fall, at a local children's musical theater company. I am vocal director, and they each have small but juicy parts. It's hard but good work that serves several purposes: keeping life as normal as possible, spending time with the kids, earning money through doing what I love (though the stipend is pitiful, the kids get free tuition since I'm on staff). Rehearsals are a great distraction from yet another lawsuit—and a justification to procrastinate breaking up with Brian.

Cheri, my lawyer, tells me that Bonnie has hired a real hard-ass attorney. His arrogance is so legendary that many local attorneys won't accept a case if he's the opposing counsel.

"I'll take him on," Cheri declares. "Let's do this." She sees my shoulders sag, my apprehension, knows what a toll the past three and a half years have taken. I am so *over* struggling. Cheri leans across her desk. "I'll fight for you and Hannah and Joshie, Rachel. We won't back down."

In all of the other cases—personal injury, workers' comp, conservatorship, I felt like part of the team. We were the victims, the good guys. Now it's me against them—David, Bonnie, and Mr. Hardass, Esq.

I tell the kids about the divorce. The subject's come up before, but I want them to know that it will be happening and will likely take a year to work out the details.

"Are you going to marry Brian?" Joshie asks.

"I'm not sure yet, buddy." I don't want them to know yet that it probably won't happen.

"OK. I kinda hope so. He takes me to McDonald's a lot." Joshie claps a hand to his mouth. "Oops—I wasn't supposed to tell you."

I'd suspected as much but hadn't said anything. Brian knows better. No wonder both of them are gaining weight. Joshie is in the pudgy nine-year-old stage. I'm trying to improve his diet, which currently, at his preference, consists mainly of white food—French fries, pasta, bread.

"Can I go jump on the trampoline now?"

Joshie runs out the back door. We'd inherited a neighbors' trampoline. It has a net, but still makes me anxious.

"Be careful!" I call after him uselessly.

Hannah has been quiet. "Mommy . . ." She is eleven but still calls me mommy. I like it. "Mommy, if Daddy hadn't been in the plane crash, would you still be married to him?"

Out of the mouths of babes. I hesitate. She doesn't know about Mark. (I planned to tell her when she gets older. Or before she reads my memoir. Need-to-know basis.)

She deserves an honest answer to this one, though. "I don't know, honey. Probably not."

We both sit for a moment, thinking about what our lives would be like if Cylinder Number Six had stayed fixed in place. If Daddy's brain hadn't been bashed in.

I open my arms, and she comes into them.

· — ·— · — — · ·

Bonnie is working quickly. As promised to Dora, she finds a furnished apartment in San Jose and plans to move David there. "It's new, pretty nice," she tells me. "Two bedrooms. Maybe the kids can spend the night sometimes. There's a Chipotle in walking distance. And a park for the kids."

"Park" is a stretch. It turns out to be a slide and some swings. It might be good for Joshie, for about five minutes.

"What about a caregiver?" I ask.

"I'm working with an agency. It's not easy to find someone who has experience with brain injuries."

I remember what Dr. Winegardner had told me over two years ago: Good caregivers are hard to find—and harder to retain. It's not my problem now. I didn't yet know how right Dr. Winegardner was. David would have a succession of caregivers over the next year, mostly Filipina women. He fired all of them. They were too stupid, he'd say. They didn't speak English well enough. They didn't let him do what he wanted—like sleep until noon, which caused him to miss appointments.

David has been growing angrier. He complains, lashes out more, is less compliant. He's never violent, but I sense the negative shift.

Not my problem. But it still worries me. I want David's living situation in San Jose to work out so he can maintain a relationship with the kids. I want him to be happy. If not happy, at least content. If he isn't to have a normal life, let him have stability, some sense of control in his own place. Not surrounded by erratic TBI patients.

Dora comes to visit in time to see the kids in *Oliver!* She stays with David in his new apartment, assessing the situation. How hard should she continue to push for him to move to Israel?

We don't discuss the future. Now that David is out of Learning Services, we are civil, even cordial. Our exchanges are superficial: logistics, the kids' schoolwork, what she'll cook for dinner. No reference to the past three and a half horrible years, Gabi, my boyfriend, my abdication of responsibility. We're both moving on. I'm grateful.

- — · — · — — · —

As part of the divorce agreement I'm required to see an employment counselor to evaluate my earning capacity, to establish the support I could get from David's estate. I go, though I'm a bit humiliated. Who the hell is this stranger to advise me? What does she know about me and my skills? Haven't I been taking care of our finances all alone these past years, establishing my own, growing business teaching singing?

I swallow my pride. I patiently explain that cantorial work is mostly nights and weekends, very difficult with the kids. We discuss options. She'll do some research and get back to me.

She calls a few days later with the conclusion that I should pursue a teaching credential so I can work as a choir director in schools. The salary won't be much at first, but it would be steady income, with benefits. Getting a credential is a path I've already considered. The stability is appealing.

Ah, benefits. The magic word. Obamacare hasn't been established yet, and I'd been struggling with increasing medical insurance payments. I haven't put a penny into retirement since the accident. A real job could have its perks.

I think about my current voice students. "I like high school age," I tell the counselor. "Of course, one-on-one is different from a whole group of them . . ."

"You'll have to get a single-subject credential, pass the CBEST exam in music. And California has upped the credential requirements—it will likely take a few years. You could probably do at least some of it online."

I agree to consider it, though the idea of going back to school—exams, writing papers, studying—is daunting. Plus, how would I pay for it?

"David's estate could cover educational costs. It's a common request and is usually granted."

I tell her I'll think about it.

. — .— . — — .

Cheri and I meet with a mediator, Mr. Hardass, and Bonnie in a small airless room in an old, dingy government building in downtown San Jose. We're supposed to try to reach some agreements. Custody is no issue, and they have agreed to let me keep the car and the Willow Glen house. Everyone agrees that stability is crucial for Hannah and Joshie. They are willing to pay for my schooling to get the credential. Check that one off the list.

Child and spousal support are different matters entirely.

Cheri, in her power suit, is geared for battle. "We're not sure how long it will take . . . remember Rachel's still working and raising the children alone. So her support needs are significant. Her income is insufficient to support her family."

Bonnie nods but Mr. Hardass's eyes narrow. "She could take more students."

Above his comb-overed head there is a clock on the wall just like the ones in the classrooms I grew up in in the '60s—a big white face, black numbers. I focus on the red second hand, tick, tick. 4:15 and 10 seconds. 4:15 and 20 seconds. I'm afraid if I take my eyes off the clock I'll explode.

Seriously? I teach forty students, six days a week. I had to take an afternoon off to attend this stupid meeting, losing over $250 in income. If I don't teach, I don't get paid. While you, you arrogant son of a bitch, you're making $450/hour pontificating.

Mr. HA sits back in his chair, arms folded. I notice that he wears cufflinks. Who wears cufflinks anymore? "Or she could go work at Starbucks."

What the fuck?

"Are you kidding me?" I'm yelling now. "Starbucks? Do you know what my life is like? Driving the kids everywhere, preparing meals, taking care of the house? All alone? You have no idea how hard it is! And you want me to leave my autistic son and anxious daughter, to pay for babysitters so I can work at Starbucks for $12 an hour?"

I pause to take a breath, shaking with rage. After all the struggle, the despair, I didn't know I still had the strength to defend myself. Cheri covers my hand with hers. Her touch, nurturing female flesh, calms, sends a message. *I told you he's a dick, but it will be OK. You will be OK.*

"Let's adjourn and schedule another meeting." Cheri stands up and starts collecting her papers, her laptop. Bonnie is trying to look neutral. She doesn't meet my eye, won't answer the question—*How could you hire this smug, self-serving jerk?*

I'm still shaking as we make our way through the parking lot. Cheri murmurs a few more reassuring words and drives off. I see Mr. Hardass, with his gelled comb-over and manicured nails, get into a shiny new Cadillac. He's probably going home to dinner cooked by his wife in a beautiful big house, to grandchildren he sees only when he feels like it.

I think about the unfairness of it all. The rage turns to tears as I make my way home to a cold stove.

— ·— ·— ·— ·—

Go on. I gather the courage to end my relationship with Brian. He is furious, hurls insults at me like baseballs. This only serves to justify my decision. It's frightening to face the future alone— again—but the truth feels so clear I can taste it. We are not, and never have been, good for each other.

The children are unshaken by news of the breakup—one positive effect of so much turmoil in their lives. As long as they have me, they show extraordinary resilience.

I can learn from them. And there will be one more test.

The kids and I are arriving home late from a rehearsal of *The Music Man* when the phone rings. It's Bonnie—David has tried to commit suicide. He's on a 72-hour psychiatric hold in the hospital.

This is my fault. All of the guilt, the remorse, the intense disappointment in myself, comes flooding back in a tsunami of shame. I am culpable. I should have been there for him, fully committed to his care. This wouldn't have happened, if only:

- I had loved him more.
- I had not been obsessed with another man.
- I had been less selfish.
- I had been less lazy.
- I had been more responsible.
- I had been true to my marriage vows.
- I hadn't been afraid of losing myself in the process of caring for him.
- I had the capacity to do whatever was necessary to keep him with his family.
- I hadn't resented the demands on my time and energy.

Perhaps Bonnie gave me more information that night, I don't remember. The details are sketchy. The caregiver had walked in on David holding a belt, trying to climb onto a chair.

"Daddy's in the hospital," I tell the kids as I kiss them goodnight. "Don't worry, he'll be OK. They just want to keep an eye on him for a few days."

That last part at least is the truth.

The likelihood of David moving to Israel is now virtually a certainty. Bonnie knows that the current situation isn't working. Dora, terrified by the suicide attempt, steps up her campaign again. This time I don't resist.

A tiny part of me gloats. I'm indeed justified in the decision I'd made to keep him at Learning Services. Dr. Winegardner had warned me. But mostly, I'm just sad. Sad at how the story seems to be ending. David will be halfway around the world. Seventy-five hundred miles from his children. Far less a part of their lives than he had ever been.

I imagine what it will be like:
- No more awkward visits.
- No more trying to come up with activities for all of us.
- No more constant in-my-face reminders—especially with David so angry and difficult —that he might have been better off if I had tried to care for him, keep him in the family home.
- Breaks for me when the kids travel to visit him.

I am relieved at the possibility of his leaving—and ashamed at that relief. I should prefer that my children's father is not living on another continent. *Will I ever stop feeling shame?*

The decision is made quickly. David will move to Israel, live on one of the floors in Dora's multi-level home in Rishon le

Zion, twenty minutes south of Tel Aviv. She will hire full-time caregivers. Dora will become the conservator of "the person," meaning she will have authority over his care—receiving a large monthly allowance from Bonnie, who will remain conservator of "the estate." Hannah and Joshie will visit David during the Christmas and summer holidays. Until they are old enough to travel on their own, they will go as unaccompanied minors, the airlines supplying supervision.

It takes a full year, but the final divorce agreement is hammered out, in October, 2009. Mr. Hardass had asserted that I should pay for the kids' twice-yearly flights to Israel. Even Bonnie shook her head in disbelief at that proposal. I'm granted child and spousal support, enough to keep us in our home and maintain our status quo—at least until the kids turn eighteen. Some matters are left unresolved. Will the kids be cut off when they become adults? Who will pay for college? There's uncertainty, but at least David will be in good hands. With family.

I hope Dora can handle it. I know I couldn't.

．—．—．—．—．

I remember David's Valentine's Day proposal, so long ago. The perfect diamond ring still sits on the bottom of my jewelry box. It's time to for it to move on. Save it for Hannah? But I'd planned to give her Mom's diamond ring for high school graduation. It represents the dreams of young love. I can't let it go.

I find a local jeweler to add a circlet of tiny diamonds surrounding my perfect simple stone. I wear that pendant constantly. It alleviates the guilt—a companion more constant since the accident. It keeps a part of David with me. The good part, the part that was whole.

A year later, in that moment of thoughtlessness after an X-ray, I throw it away.

I often wonder what I would have done if it had been Hannah or Joshie who had needed care. What if one of them had been born with Down syndrome or some other developmental disability? What if Joshie had been severely autistic? If Hannah had hurt her head falling off a bike or scooter, had irreparable brain damage?

Those awful imaginings—what would I do *if*—never include purely physical disabilities. I like to think I could handle paralysis, loss of a limb, a chronic disease.

Mental impairment is in a different category.

In my fantasies I rally, doing whatever it takes to provide the best care necessary, no matter the sacrifice.

I hope I'm never tested on those circumstances. It's an untenable situation, to be thrust into the role of caregiver. For Dora, though she still struggles to find balance after all these years, it's a role she's equipped to handle. I had to learn that I was not.

I'm one of the lucky ones. I had options. David's injury occurred on the job so workers' comp covered his medical needs. I had access to good lawyers who found deep pockets to pursue. We owned a house, a car. We had a caring, supportive family and community. I'm brutally aware that many who are forced into a caretaking position have no choices.

I still carry guilt. It sparks when I see my peers taking care of ill or disabled family members. I have guilt when I visit my father in his convalescent home. I have guilt whenever Hannah or Josh has a performance or graduation that David would have attended if he lived closer.

But now, after all these years, I accept my truth: I am flawed, but I'm strong. I'm selfish, but generous. I can break down, but I am resilient.

Like David, I'm a survivor.

Epilogue

AUGUST, 2012

"Mom!" Both kids run to hug me first, carrying backpacks and dragging big suitcases. I'm used to the SFO International Terminal meeting area—exhausted travelers released from customs to the arms of excited relatives.

They chatter excitedly on the moving walkway, burning off the adrenaline rush of release from the confinement of the four-teen-hour flight from Tel Aviv. They're exploding with stories about their Dad and cousins, Dora's cooking, summer camp in northern Israel.

"We couldn't swim in the ocean," Josh complains. He's thirteen and insists on dropping the "ie" in his name. "Because there were jellyfish. But we had fun anyway."

We drive south down Interstate 280, the hills dry and golden, the reservoir predictably low. They're quiet, absorbed in cell phones that didn't work well overseas.

I glance in the rearview mirror. Josh is bronzed, hair a little blonder. Is it possible to grow two inches in two weeks? Though his body is screaming adolescence, he's still a little boy. His high, unchanged voice looks mismatched with broad shoulders. He's not as tall as his sister yet, but there's a foreshadow of a solid frame to come.

Hannah sitting next to me is also tanned, light brown hair in a loose pony, taller than me. She is fifteen, part woman. A small part. She'll still crawl into my bed needing closeness, a hug, reassurance that I'm there no matter what. Reassurance that I will not go to work one day and never come home.

The two-week breaks I get when they visit their Dad are blissful. This time I attend a writing retreat on the North Coast, do some dating, eat what I want when I want. But I'm ready to have them back.

"Mom." Hannah looks up from her phone. "Really good news. Aunt Tina and Uncle Sigi want you to come to Joel's Bar Mitzvah in December."

"Really?" I'm astonished. The contact I've had with them since the plane crash has been minimal. They've let Dora do the dirty work. Now they want *me* to come to their son's Bar Mitzvah in Munich?

"Yep!" says Hannah. "I think you should come. Aunt Dora does, too." She turns back to her phone.

My evil twin starts the tirade. *You're seriously considering it? You can't go. They're inviting you just to be nice, but don't delude yourself. They're still pissed at you for abandoning David. You'll have to face all of David's childhood friends, maybe even Jossi and Gabi. You'll get dirty looks. That Munich Jewish community is so tight, so bonded. Everyone will know that the evil witch is in town. You'll be the subject of nasty gossip. Don't go.*

Shut the fuck up, I retort. *You are toxic. I no longer have to listen to you. I'm not proud of what I did, but I'm not ashamed either. I've accepted my limitations, my flaws, and my strengths. I made the best decisions I could. This is my life.*

I will face them, head held high.

I'm not ashamed.

"So, want to look at flights when we get home?"

- —.—.— —.

Four months later we are in a ritzy hotel ballroom in downtown Munich. I've been seated next to Joel's piano teacher and his husband. We have a lively conversation (they're sweet about indulging my attempt to practice German) about Mozart and Chopin and commiserate about the challenges of teaching music.

I look across the room at the head table: David, our children, Sigi and Dora's families. On the periphery, I feel a small pang of sadness. But I am in the room. I've been included.

I see David is relaxed, happy to be surrounded by his kids, his family. I walk over.

"Hey David."

He turns toward me and smiles.

I ask, "Wanna dance?"

Santorini, Greece, Summer 2018

Postscript

DAVID LIVES IN ISRAEL WITH A full-time caregiver he loves, Teresita, in a large duplex next to Dora and Rafi. He uses their in-home gym, sleeps a lot, and spends time on the computer. The kids still visit about once a year.

Josh is studying business at Chapman University in Orange, California. When he's not studying or choreographing fraternity skits, he DJs weddings, graduation parties and Bar and Bat Mitzvah receptions. He's also an expert break dancer with a mean head spin.

Hannah graduated Purdue University in Indiana with a degree in Retail Management/Fashion Merchandising. After a trip through Israel and Europe, she's now working in her dream field of sustainable fashion. She still dances but no longer wears princess dresses.

I remarried—a physicist, Richard—who's busy discovering the secrets of the universe. We love hiking in the hills above Stanford University with our two dogs, Nala and Beenie, and going to opera and the theater. I still perform occasionally but mostly spend my time gardening, cooking, and training the next generation of singers.

We're all alright.

Acknowledgments

MANY THANKS TO MY VILLAGE, AND to those who turned my dream of writing *Crash* into reality:

- Laura Davis, writing teacher and author extraordinaire, whose gentle wisdom and craft laid the foundation for skills previously untapped;
- David Colin Carr, whose editing pen was wielded with love and encouragement;
- Susan Brown, who helped give my early work shape and direction;
- Writing friends Amanda Cavin Bell, Tawnya Bragg, Vanya Erickson, Eileen Tejada, Mary Ashley, Nancy and Glen Brown, Stacey Saadi, and Lisa Deverse, for being an integral part of my creative, loving community;
- Nora Rousso for her friendship and legal advice;
- Attorney Steve Ellenberg, for helping me feel safe when I didn't;
- Angela Cesena, speech and language pathologist, for her expertise;

- Brooke Warner—publisher, Samantha Strom—project manager, Julie Metz—cover design, and Tabitha Lahr—interior design and the whole team at SheWrites Press for believing in my story and supporting this first-time author;
- Publicist Caitlin Hamilton Summie and her team for getting *Crash* out into the world,
- Alicia Telfer for her photography skills, website and social media know-how;
- Beta readers: Francine Falk-Allen, Susie Turner, Paul Hettler, Lisa Deverse, Karen Hammer, Jessica Braverman-Birch, Dina Jacobson, and Lisa Hettler-Smith for reading the earliest draft;
- Rabbi Dana Magat of Temple Emanu-El in San Jose, for, well—everything;
- Friends, family, and synagogue communities of Temple Emanu-El, Congregation Sinai and Yavneh Day School who supported me during those awful years—schlepping kids, providing meals, childcare and hugs, and lifting me up when I couldn't stand on my own. I am eternally grateful and will never forget your kindness;
- Hannah and Josh(ie), who gave me permission to tell their stories;
- Richard, who supported my crazy dream;
- Dora, who gave David a home when I couldn't.

It truly takes a village. Thank you.

About the Author

RACHEL MICHELBERG grew up in the San Francisco Bay Area and still enjoys living there with her husband Richard and their two dogs, Nala and Beenie. She earned her bachelor of music degree in vocal performance from San José State University and has performed leading roles in musicals and opera from *Carmen* to Eliza Doolittle in *My Fair Lady* and the Mother Abbess (three times!) in *The Sound of Music*. When Rachel isn't working with one of her thirty voice and piano students, she loves gardening, hiking, and making her own bone broth. *Crash: How I Became a Reluctant Caregiver* is her first book.

Author photo © Alicia Telfer

SELECTED TITLES FROM SHE WRITES PRESS

She Writes Press is an independent publishing
company founded to serve women writers everywhere.
Visit us at www.shewritespress.com.

Edna's Gift: How My Broken Sister Taught Me to Be Whole
by Susan Rudnick. $16.95, 9781631525155. The story of
how Susan Rudnick's maddening—yet endearing—mentally
challenged sister became her greatest life teacher.

Green Nails and Other Acts of Rebellion: Life After Loss by
Elaine Soloway. $16.95, 978-1-63152-919-1. An honest, often
humorous account of the joys and pains of caregiving for a
loved one with a debilitating illness.

*The Buddha at My Table: How I Found Peace in Betrayal and
Divorce* by Tammy Letherer. $16.95, On a Tuesday night, just
before Christmas, after he had put their three children in bed,
Tammy Letherer's husband shattered her world and destroyed
every assumption she'd ever made about love, friendship, and
faithfulness. In the aftermath of this betrayal, however, she
finds unexpected blessings—and, ultimately, the path to
freedom.

Off the Rails: One Family's Journey Through Teen Addiction by
Susan Burrowes. $16.95, 978-1-63152-467-7. An inspiring
story of family love, determination, and the last-resort intervention that helped one troubled young woman find sobriety
after a terrifying and harrowing journey.

Her Beautiful Brain: A Memoir by Ann Hedreen. $16.95,
978-1-93831-492-6. The heartbreaking story of a daughter's
experiences as her beautiful, brainy mother begins to lose her
mind to an unforgiving disease: Alzheimer's.